Access Your Online Resources

Word Aware 3 is accompanied by a number of printable online materials, indicated by this icon designed to ensure this resource best supports your professional needs. To make maximum use of this resource download the online resources. **There are more resources available online than are printed in the book.**

Activate your online resources:

Go to www.routledge.com/cw/speechmark and click on the cover of this book

Click the 'Sign in or Request Access' button and follow the instructions in order to access the resources

Word Aware 3 is a comprehensive, practical and engaging resource that focuses on teaching vocabulary and word learning skills to children aged 6 to 11 years who have vocabulary learning needs.

For many children, particularly those with Special Educational Needs and Disabilities (SEND) or those whose home language isn't English (ELL or EAL learners), the vocabulary of the classroom can be a barrier to learning. This book outlines how to best support these children who require extra help, offering concrete, easy-to-implement activities and resources for use in small groups, to maximise the impact on learning and open up access to the curriculum.

Word Aware 3:

- Takes a highly practical, evidence-based and curriculum-focused approach to vocabulary learning that supports a broad range of learners

- Includes photocopiable and downloadable planning, intervention and evaluation resources

- Provides staff training resources and an overview video presented by the authors

This book can be used as an adjunct to *Word Aware 1*, or as an intervention on its own. Although it is most suited to children aged 6 to 11 years, it may be adapted for older students with significant learning needs. It is an essential resource for teaching assistants and learning support assistants and will also save time for Special Educational Needs Co-ordinators (SENCOs) and Speech and Language Therapists (SaLTs) who are keen to establish effective vocabulary interventions.

Anna Branagan is a Speech and Language Therapist. In Gloucestershire, Anna works within a Youth Support Team supporting vulnerable young people. In Worcestershire, she works within mainstream schools supporting inclusive practice. Anna trained at Leeds Metropolitan University 25 years ago. She is the co-author of bestselling Speechmark resources *Language for Thinking* (second edition, 2017), *Word Aware 1* (second edition, 2022), *Word Aware 2* (2017) and *Language for Behaviour and Emotions* (2020).

Stephen Parsons is a Speech and Language Therapist, trainer and author of practical language development resources for teachers and Speech and Language Therapists (SaLTs). From 1996–2017, Stephen worked as a Speech and Language Therapy Service Manager in Hackney and the City of London. With over 30 years' experience in the field, he is co-author of bestselling Speechmark resources *Language for Thinking* (second edition, 2017), *Word Aware 1* (second edition, 2022), *Word Aware 2* (2017) and

Language for Behaviour and Emotions (2020). Stephen graduated in Speech Pathology from Flinders University before attaining an MSc in Speech and Language Therapy from City University, London, in 2000. He currently serves as Chair of NAPLIC, the UK association for professionals working with children and young people with developmental language disorder.

Teaching Vocabulary in Small Groups for Ages 6 to 11

Anna Branagan and Stephen Parsons

Routledge
Taylor & Francis Group

LONDON AND NEW YORK

First published 2022
by Routledge
2 Park Square, Milton Park, Abingdon, Oxon OX14 4RN

and by Routledge
605 Third Avenue, New York, NY 10158

Routledge is an imprint of the Taylor & Francis Group, an informa business

British Library Cataloguing-in-Publication Data
A catalogue record for this book is available from the British Library

Library of Congress Cataloging-in-Publication Data
Names: Branagan, Anna, author. | Parsons, Stephen, author.
Title: Word aware 3 : teaching vocabulary in small groups for ages 5 to 11
    / Anna Branagan and Stephen Parsons.
Other titles: Word aware three
Description: Abingdon, Oxon ; New York, NY : Routledge,
    2021. | Includes bibliographical references.
Identifiers: LCCN 2021008564 (print) | LCCN 2021008565 (ebook) | ISBN 9780367747534 (hardback) |
    ISBN 9780367747558 (paperback) | ISBN 9781003159377 (ebook)
Subjects: LCSH: Vocabulary—Study and teaching (Elementary) | Language arts
    (Elementary) | Group work in education. | English language—Remedial
    teaching. | Students with disabilities—Education.
Classification: LCC LB1574.5 .B69 2021 (print) | LCC LB1574.5 (ebook) |
    DDC 372.44—dc23
LC record available at https://lccn.loc.gov/2021008564
LC ebook record available at https://lccn.loc.gov/2021008565

ISBN: 978–0-367–74753–4 (hbk)
ISBN: 978–0-367–74755–8 (pbk)
ISBN: 978–1-003–15937–7 (ebk)

DOI: 10.4324/9781003159377

Typeset in Berthold Akzidenz Grotesk
by Apex CoVantage, LLC

Printed in the UK by Severn, Gloucester on responsibly sourced paper

Access the companion website: www.routledge.com/cw/speechmark

To Kevin and Steve, without whom none of this would be possible.

To all the children and young people with vocabulary learning needs who we have worked with. We have learnt so much from you. We hope our collated knowledge will go on and help many more.

Contents

Preface

Understanding the meaning of words and using words to talk about the world is a fundamental skill for all learners. However, there are children in our classrooms for whom this process does not come easily. They may enter school with a comparatively limited vocabulary, and as the demands of the curriculum increase, the words they need to know become an insurmountable barrier. The vocabulary learning difficulty impacts on learning and self-image.

These children may have labels such as Developmental Language Disorder, Down Syndrome, Dyslexia, Attention Deficit Hyperactivity Disorder (ADHD) and learning difficulties, or no label at all. What they share is not being able to learn words in the classroom the way their typically developing peers do.

This book outlines how to support children who have additional vocabulary learning needs, and who need extra support. The approach is focused on the classroom, as this provides a rich word learning environment. Every effort should be made to develop word learning in the classroom in a way that supports a broad range of learners. Once this is established, children with higher level vocabulary needs can be supported via in class strategies and small group interventions, if required. To be successful, teachers, support staff and families need to work together to a common goal.

This book has been developed by analysing research and best practice in this field and translating it into practical, easy to implement activities. Guidance and resources, including staff training are provided within this book and the accompanying companion website.

The companion website is accessible via: www.routledge.com/cw/speechmark

It includes printable colour copies of planning, intervention and evaluation resources as well as a training video delivered by the authors.

The *Word Aware* Series

There are now three books in the *Word Aware* series. Each has a different focus, but they all work together.

Word Aware 1: outlines a whole class, whole school approach for teaching vocabulary to all learners aged 5 to 11 years.

Word Aware 2: is also a whole class approach, but the target age range is 3 to 5 years.

Word Aware 3: works in partnership with *Word Aware 1* to support children aged 6 to 11 years who have vocabulary learning needs.

The three books provide a cohesive package that can be used flexibly to support primary/elementary learners. To create a fully comprehensive vocabulary offer for your children, start with *Word Aware 2*, so that vulnerable word learners do not fall behind in their first years of school. Build on this with *Word Aware 1* to ensure there is optimum vocabulary teaching across the school, and then implement support for the most vulnerable word learners with this book, *Word Aware 3*.

Stephen Parsons and Anna Branagan

References

Parsons, S. & Branagan, A. (2022) *Word Aware 1: Teaching Vocabulary Across the Day, Across the Curriculum*, 2nd edition. Abingdon, Oxon: Routledge.

Parsons, S. & Branagan, A. (2017) *Word Aware 2: Teaching Vocabulary in the Early Years.* London: Speechmark.

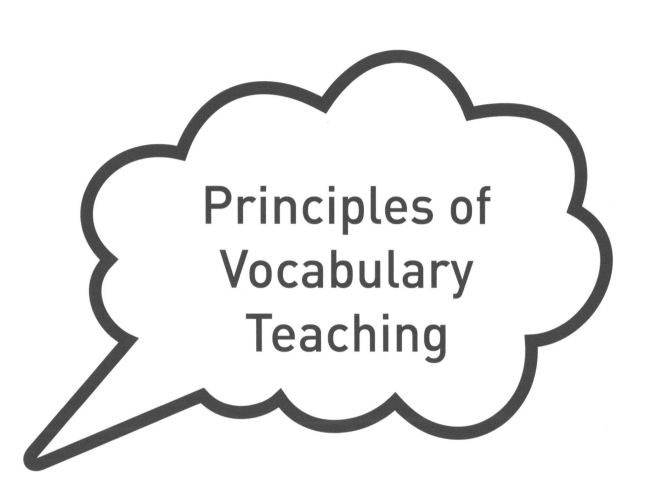

Principles of Vocabulary Teaching

Chapter 1. Principles of Vocabulary Teaching

Key Points

1. Vocabulary is important for learning, for accessing the curriculum, and also reading and writing.
2. The average student learns an estimated seven words per day every day they are in education.
3. There may be a very large 'word gap' between children with vocabulary needs and their peers.
4. Developing spoken language also develops reading and writing.
5. There are many children in our classrooms with vocabulary learning needs, for all manner of reasons.
6. Vocabulary teaching needs to be embedded in the classroom, and any withdrawal support needs to be curriculum-focused.

Principles

These points are important for all children but are particularly important for those with vocabulary learning needs.

1. A whole school approach
2. A multifaceted approach
3. Explicitly teach words
4. Multiple exposures
5. Teach words in context
6. Link spoken and written vocabulary
7. Analyse elements of words
8. Go with the child (at the right rate)
9. Get excited about words
10. Teach strategies
11. Work in partnership with families

These are all based upon research which is further expanded on in Chapter 6. In addition, they are based upon research which is given in more detail in Chapter 1 of *Word Aware 1*, 2nd edition. This is available to download from the Speechmark companion website at www.routledge.com/cw/speechmark

What We Mean by 'Vocabulary'

This book is all about vocabulary, so we need to start by defining what we mean by 'vocabulary'. 'Vocabulary' refers to the collection of words that we use to communicate with one another. The words may be spoken or written (or signed), but they convey meaning. To be able to understand what others are saying to us or have written, we need to be able to understand the meaning of the words. The first words that young children learn are concrete nouns like 'banana' or those which fulfil needs, such as 'more', but as children develop the number of words increases dramatically and they start to use words to represent abstract concepts such as 'together', 'within', and 'peace', as well as emotions.

Vocabulary Is Important

To put it simply, to access learning, children need words. In the classroom a student will not get far in mathematics if they do not understand what 'division' means or in science if they do not understand 'habitats'. Vocabulary is important for accessing the content of the curriculum. Deep understanding of words such as 'partitioning', 'fact', 'polygon', 'hypothesis', 'respect' and 'consequence' will open up new ways of thinking for children. We call these words 'verbal concepts' and they are particularly important for learning. The challenge is that verbal concepts are often the hardest words for children to get a hold of.

Vocabulary is also linked to literacy. Stories contain a huge range of words, many of which we are less likely to use when we talk to each other. One small excerpt from *James and the Giant Peach* (Dahl, 1961) at the beginning of Chapter 2 contains less common words such as 'oozing', 'overwhelmed', 'glared', 'peculiar', 'brute', 'hobbled' and 'mildewed'. Not every one of these words is needed to understand the story but being able to understand 'overwhelmed by his own unhappiness' gives a greater insight into James's feelings. He is not just unhappy; he is overwhelmed by it. The flipside of reading is of course writing. A story written with limited vocabulary is usually rather dull. To write well, children need a range of words at the forefront of their minds. Writing engagingly requires a large, sophisticated vocabulary that can be used meaningfully.

So Many Words to Learn

English contains an estimated one million words. Luckily, most of these are not in use, but most adults can understand somewhere between 30,000 to 50,000 words. That is still a big number, and most of those words are learnt during children's time in school. To get to the 30,000 figure requires children to learn seven words per day, every day for their entire schooling. For most children, simple exposure to a rich vocabulary from home and school is enough to learn words. They will learn from bedtime stories; they will learn from peers in the playground; they will learn during assembly; and they will even learn words at the supermarket. Of course, specific teaching of words will help, but most words will still be learnt via exposure. Do not try and teach seven words per day. It is simply not possible.

Word Gap

The so-called 'word gap' has received a great deal of attention in recent years. Rightly so, as a great number of teachers are concerned about those children who do not have the words they need to access learning. Without attention, the word gap grows and grows, and its impact on learning becomes more significant. Children with poor vocabulary quite often struggle to learn to read, and even when they do, they may not understand what they decode. As a result, they are less likely to read for pleasure, which in turn means they are exposed to less vocabulary, which means their vocabulary growth rate is slow, which in turn impacts on their reading and so on.

Some children are seemingly born talking and take to reading effortlessly. They are likely to live in highly verbal and literate households, so they hear and read lots of words. They may be in a class with a child who has been much slower to develop language, struggled to learn to read and whose family do not use talk in the same way. There is a huge word gap between these two children, and without attention it can become a learning gap.

There is no magic pill which will enable the second child to catch up and close the word gap. Instead, we need to be smart and teach important words for learning and thus reduce the impact of the word gap. And because of the sheer number of words, vocabulary teaching needs to be a long-term process.

Spoken Language Is the Foundation of Reading

'Literacy floats on a sea of talk' (Britton, 1970) is an old but valuable quote as it highlights the often-overlooked role that spoken language has to play in the development of reading. Children with well-developed spoken language skills are far more likely to become good readers, as knowing lots of words supports their development of phonological awareness skills (needed for phonics), along with the ability to make sense of what they have read. As children's reading skills develop, their comprehension of what they have read is developed through discussion about the text with others, and then later by their own internal monologue. By constantly asking themselves questions in their head, they deepen understanding. And even though this skill is done silently and often subconsciously, it is still based in spoken language.

Even for children who can decode well, written words on the page are problematic because they need to be fully understood before they come to life. Even pictures in books only provide a little information. Spoken words have the advantage of coming with lots of extra information such as tone of voice, facial expression and gesture, as well as physical and social contexts. There is also the option of asking the speaker if the listener has not understood. Take our *James and the Giant Peach* (Dahl, 1961) example from earlier, when James was 'overwhelmed by his own unhappiness'. If read independently, the child needs to understand each word before building the meaning. If, however, the text was being read to the class by an animated teacher, the phrase could be accompanied by a sad face, downward intonation and a sigh, all of which would provide important information to support comprehension. If your friend described themselves as being 'overwhelmed by his own unhappiness' you would have even more to go on, as you will know about their personality, background and recent events. Words heard in real contexts come with so much more information than words on the page.

To write meaningfully, children need to know lots of words well before they can construct them into sentences, and then into paragraphs and longer. Their ability to build sentences and text, once again starts with spoken language. Children cannot write what they cannot speak.

Spoken language is important to the development of reading, and so children with less- developed spoken language skills need to have their literacy development carefully monitored and supported.

Children with Word Learning Needs

Word learning difficulties are either as a result of the environment or within child factors, or both. By environment we mean the words that children are exposed to. This starts off at home, but includes childcare and school too, and for older children independent reading. The home environment is where the journey starts, and so it is important. But even the most educated homes use simple vocabulary on an average day, and so whilst important, the home environment is not the sole contributor. Equally, many families do not appreciate how important they are within the word learning process, but by involving them they can get engaged in the process and really make a difference. It can be as simple as encouraging families to read to their children, because books generally contain more varied and complex vocabulary than the words we use when we talk to one another.

Within child factors are the individual's word learning capacity. It can sometimes feel a little uncomfortable thinking this way, but some children will find word learning harder than others. This should not limit our view of children's potential, but rather guide how we teach words to them. There is naturally a range, and some conditions such as Developmental Language Disorder, Down Syndrome, dyslexia and learning disabilities may directly impact on word learning, although within each group this will also vary from child to child. Children with word learning needs often need to hear words more times before they learn them, and they may also need to be shown how to use new words more explicitly. With a few small changes to vocabulary teaching, children at higher risk of vocabulary learning needs can learn new words too.

In training sessions run by the authors, attendees quite often mention that English as an additional language (EAL) learners/English Language Learners (ELL) have vocabulary learning difficulties. It is very important to stress that having a home language different from the school language does not negatively impact on vocabulary. In the early stages, vocabulary learning may be slower in each individual language, but long-term there are many EAL learners who go on to have advanced vocabularies. EAL learners will experience varied home environments and within child factors, just the same as their monolingual peers. The message to families from professionals should be clear: a strong home language will support long-term vocabulary growth in the school language as well. If parents' English is limited, home to school communication may be impacted, but working closely with families and the community to develop children's home language will pay dividends.

A Tiered Approach

Vocabulary is important in all subjects and for all learners and so needs to be a focus in the classroom. This is expanded on in *Word Aware 1*, 2nd edition (Parsons & Branagan, 2022) and its early years equivalent *Word Aware 2* (Parsons & Branagan, 2017).

Even with a focus on vocabulary in the classroom, some children will need extra support. This is expanded on in the next chapter, but to be truly effective, extra support for vocabulary must be linked to the curriculum and what is being taught in class. Words are learnt by hearing them in context lots of times and much of that happens as a part of regular teaching. That can be built on with more repetition and learning opportunities happening as part of the intervention. By working in tandem and supporting the curriculum, children with vocabulary learning needs can learn curriculum-related vocabulary. Knowing these words then increases their access to whole class teaching, which in turn benefits their inclusion, and in our experience develops their self-esteem and motivation. This book provides support and guidance to support the children who need extra support to access the curriculum.

There will be a third set of children: those who have more severe vocabulary needs. These are children who have significant language learning needs and require highly specific teaching. This support would typically be provided by Speech and Language Therapists/Pathologists or specialist teachers. This book may still be used with this group of children, but it will need to be tailored under the guidance of a specialist.

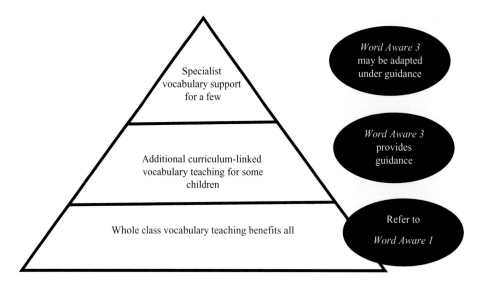

Word Aware Principles

Word Aware is built upon the following principles, all of which are based upon research and good classroom practice. The principles apply to all children but require a slightly different emphasis and application when it comes to supporting children with vocabulary learning needs.

Principle 1: A whole school approach

The curriculum provides a huge range of vocabulary learning opportunities. The wide range of words that are encountered in whole class books, and the specific vocabulary contained in maths, science, geography and history all provide children with opportunities to learn words. Every subject, every topic, every book comes with its own vocabulary.

Because there are so many words to learn, vocabulary needs a long-term effort. One teacher or teaching assistant on their own cannot make enough difference. It needs a team effort, year on year.

The authors have written in detail about this in *Word Aware 1*, 2nd edition (Parsons & Branagan, 2022) and *Word Aware 2* (Parsons & Branagan, 2017).

For children with vocabulary learning needs the focus should still be the classroom.

Principle 2: A multifaceted approach

Words are everywhere and reflect every aspect of life. There are short but powerful verbs such as 'crush', luscious adjectives such as 'opulent' and complex ideas represented by words such as 'civilisation'. These cannot all be learnt via one simple method. Children come in all shapes and sizes too and have different learning profiles and interests. Therefore, we need to have flexible approaches which reflect all the types of words and the full range of learners.

Children with vocabulary learning needs often have difficulties accessing classroom talk. By giving them opportunities in the small group to have more hands-on opportunities with new words will support their learning, especially when accompanied by a dialogue between the group facilitator and child.

Principle 3: Explicitly teach words

Choosing words that are at the right level is the important first step, but then teaching them in a multi-sensory manner gives all children a boost. This is a key component of *Word Aware* and should be part of whole class teaching.

For children with vocabulary learning needs this process needs to be expanded and more focused. They need to:

• go through each step methodically,

• hear the word used in more sentences to show them how to use it,

• have stronger sensory experiences to understand the meaning,

• have more support with understanding how it fits with their life experiences, and then

• have more opportunities to encounter the word, so it is not forgotten.

Structured pre-teaching including the above elements gives children a boost before they go into the classroom. The word is already partly learnt, so in class they are finishing off the process rather than playing catch up. For children who struggle to access whole class teaching, going into class with some learning under their belt increases their chances of accessing what is going on. This has knock-on effects on learning, attention, engagement and identity as a learner.

Principle 4: Multiple exposures

To learn words, children need to hear them lots of times. To start with they are not aware of the word, then they become aware of it, and as they hear it more times they gradually pick up on its meaning. Once they understand what it means and use it, most children retain words well.

Children with vocabulary learning needs take longer at each step, but in particular they have difficulties with embedding the word and retaining it. To overcome this, they need to hear the word two to three times more than their typically developing peers. They also need more opportunities to come back and revisit the word.

Principle 5: Teach words in context

Words are always much more than what is written in a dictionary. A dictionary is obviously a good place to start, but we learn about how to use words by hearing how other people use words. So, teaching children dictionary definitions just won't cut it. Children need to hear words being used in ways that are meaningful.

Children with vocabulary learning needs may require extra support in making the links between words and the context in which they are being used. They may need more examples of contexts so they can apply the word in more than just one situation. Extra thought will also need to be given to how the word is going to be learnt and used outside of the group.

Principle 6: Link spoken and written vocabulary

Words are spoken and written, so it cannot be one or the other, it needs to be both. When we hear someone say a word, we get extra information from facial expression, voice, gesture as well as the physical clues such as what we can see and touch. We get none of this when we read a word. If we are lucky, we might have an accompanying picture. With spoken words we can also have a conversation with the speaker and learn more about the word. So spoken words are generally easier to learn, especially for children at the early stages of word learning. For typically developing children who read widely, reading eventually becomes the main source of word learning as books contain more advanced vocabulary.

For children with vocabulary learning needs to make explicit links between what they read and what they hear, simply talk about words they are reading. This brings the word to life and deepens understanding.

Principle 7: Analyse elements of words

Words can be broken down into speech sounds (phonemes). For instance: although we write four letters for 'fish', we hear three speech sounds: 'f', 'i' and 'sh'. Emphasising speech sounds helps all word learners, but will be particularly useful for those who have vocabulary learning needs.

Words can also be broken down into prefix, suffix and base or root. For instance: in the word 'disagreeable,' 'dis' is the prefix, 'able' is the suffix and 'agree' is the root or base word. This is a sophisticated skill, but it is important for vocabulary growth because once children can identify patterns in words, they can learn many new words themselves.

Children with vocabulary learning needs will particularly benefit from being specifically taught these skills that their peers may pick up naturally. For vulnerable learners, the teaching will need to be more systematic, with more examples and more opportunities to apply their knowledge.

Principle 8: Go with the child (at the right rate)

If children already know the words they are being taught then they will not learn anything new. If the words being taught are too challenging or the style of teaching is too advanced, then teaching time is also wasted. This is true for every child.

But it is doubly true for children with vocabulary learning needs. Sometimes there is talk about 'teaching to the top'. It is good to have high expectations, but if this means talking over children's heads, it is a waste of time. If I attended a lecture on advanced mathematics, I would hear lots of new words, but I would not learn them, because I do not have the prerequisite learning. I would probably also end up frustrated and bored. We need to pitch our teaching at the right level to have maximum impact and make the best use of precious time.

There is also no point going too fast and feeling a pressure to teach lots of words if we are not allowing enough time for children to learn the words. Teaching needs to be at a pace that allows for in-depth learning.

Principle 9: Get excited about words

If children find words fun and interesting, they are more likely to engage with learning them. We therefore need to make word learning enjoyable. Playing games, exposing children to interesting words and showing our own enjoyment are all part of this process.

Children with vocabulary learning needs may enter our classrooms with less understanding that words can be fun or may even think that word learning is not enjoyable. Our message and our practice need to show that word learning is fun for all.

Principle 10: Teach strategies

Children learn most words independently, either from listening to others or through reading. By teaching strategies, we can greatly increase children's word learning capacity. Strategies such as using context or dictionary skills will support long-term vocabulary growth. The aim is that we want all children to see themselves as independent word learners and have a repertoire of skills they can use.

Many children with vocabulary learning needs do not even recognise when they do not understand a word, and subsequently do not ask. A simple strategy such as modelling how to ask about unknown words can have a significant impact. These skills will need to be taught methodically and opportunities for application provided.

Principle 11: Work in partnership with families

Vocabulary learning does not happen just in school, it happens at home too. Working with families will prove beneficial for all children.

Families of children with vocabulary learning needs have an even more important role to play. Their inclusion should be built into every vocabulary intervention. One issue is that many families may be wary

of 'vocabulary', as it sounds like it will be literacy-based, dry and another chore to fit into busy family life. The aim is therefore to make family involvement engaging and straightforward. It can be as simple as playing word games, reading to children and talking about words or celebrating success.

References

Britton, J. (1970). *Language and Learning*. Coral Gables, FL: University of Miami Press.

Dahl, R. (1961). *James and the Giant Peach*. New York: Puffin.

Parsons, S. & Branagan, A. (2022). *Word Aware 1: Teaching Vocabulary Across the Day, Across the Curriculum*, 2nd edition. Abingdon, Oxon: Routledge.

Parsons, S. & Branagan, A. (2017). *Word Aware 2: Teaching Vocabulary in the Early Years*. London: Speechmark.

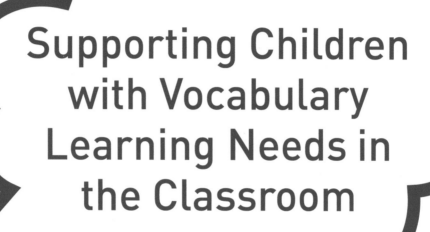

Supporting Children
with Vocabulary
Learning Needs in
the Classroom

Chapter 2. Supporting Children with Vocabulary Learning Needs in the Classroom

This chapter outlines the preparation required to successfully support children with additional vocabulary learning needs. It covers in-class support and how that works in tandem with the group intervention and home support.

The diagram below illustrates how to support children with additional vocabulary learning needs. It starts with whole class teaching of vocabulary which is built upon by adding in extra targeted strategies and finally the vocabulary group. All three levels work together and in conjunction with families.

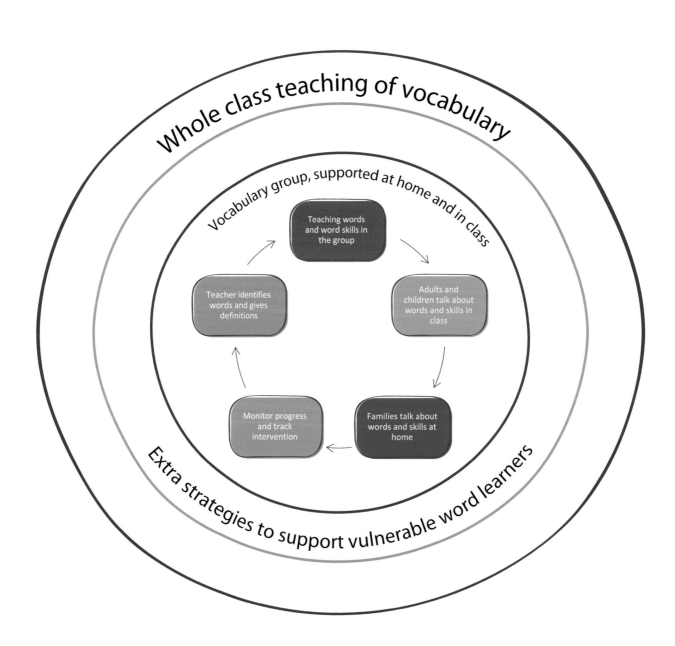

Supporting Children with Vocabulary Learning Needs in the Classroom

Many educators will be aware that vocabulary is an issue for their students and so will take the path of identifying at-risk children and giving them a boost via a short-term vocabulary group intervention outside of the classroom. Whilst well-intentioned, the impact of such a group is likely to be limited. This is because:

1. The words are unlikely to be heard enough times to be fully established;

2. Even if they are learnt in the group, they get forgotten by the next session, as the children do not hear them enough outside of the group;

3. The real context is lacking, and so children learn a one-dimensional aspect of the word. They learn what they have been told and do not really understand how the new words apply to them;

4. The learning stays in the group and is not used in the classroom. Generalisation to other contexts is particularly hard for many children with special educational needs (SEN), but out of class teaching requires them to do what they specifically struggle with;

5. There are so many words to learn, so even if children learn all of the words they are taught, it has a minimal impact on learning; and

6. There are also likely to be further issues with identifying words. Do you start with basic concepts these children are lacking or the specific words that are taught in class?

A Better Way Forward

Start with the classroom. The classroom naturally provides a rich context for word learning. A huge number of words are read and heard as part of everyday teaching. To learn words, children need to encounter them many times in meaningful ways. This happens naturally in the classroom when listening to stories, conducting science experiments, engaging in handicrafts and during whole class instruction. The richness of the curriculum provides plentiful opportunities for word learning. The approaches outlined in *Word Aware 1*, 2nd edition (Parsons & Branagan, 2022) are inclusive and adaptable to support a wide range of word learners within the classroom. These were outlined more fully in Chapter 1, but are built upon these principles:

1. A whole school approach

2. A multifaceted approach

3. Explicitly teach words

4. Multiple exposures

5. Teach words in context

6. Link spoken and written vocabulary

7. Analyse elements of words

8. Go with the child (at the right rate)

9. Get excited about words

10. Teach strategies

11. Work in partnership with families

The focus should remain on whole class teaching, as getting it right in the classroom will support all children, and for those with additional learning needs small adaptations made in the classroom will impact every day. Changing vocabulary teaching practice in the classroom requires an ongoing cycle of skill development, reflection, implementation and review. It is not a simple task and one which can be achieved easily, but as vocabulary interfaces with learning for all children it is a crucial teaching skill.

The word learning environment of the classroom has the potential to overwhelm vulnerable word learners. There are simply too many words that these children do not know and left unsupported this will impact on their learning and engagement. Small changes, when done regularly as part of standard teaching, will go a long way to supporting vulnerable word learners.

Start by being aware of the vocabulary of the classroom. Are the words children are being exposed to at the right level? The words need to be challenging, but not inaccessible. Also be aware of children's general vocabulary abilities. Vocabulary reflects children's experiences as well as their innate word learning capacity. It will vary enormously between schools, but also within the same class.

These general strategies will support all word learners, but they may be enhanced for those with vocabulary learning needs. They are in no particular order.

Action	Good practice	Extra support in the classroom for vulnerable word learners
Expectations	• High expectations for all	• Keep high expectations but be aware of each child's starting point. They can make progress with the right teaching but only if it <u>starts from the right place</u>
Teacher talk	• Know which words you want children to learn • Define new words using simple words and sentences. • Use words meaningfully and model how to use the new words	• Ensure the words are at the right challenge level. Do not presume what children know • Define the target words in short sentences using words the children know well • Use the new words in situations that children are very familiar with • Link the words to hands-on learning opportunities
Build a word learning environment	• Establish word learning tools such as Word Walls (see page 40), Word Pots (see page 83), dictionaries and thesauri • Introduce and explicitly teach their use	• Explicitly teach use of word learning tools in small steps and model their application • Prompt the use of word learning tools, such as taking a word from the word wall and putting it into writing

Supporting Children with Vocabulary Learning Needs in the Classroom

Action	Good practice	Extra support in the classroom for vulnerable word learners
Everybody is a word learner	• Establish a culture where all children see themselves as word learners on a journey to learn words and word learning skills • Highlight words that are genuinely new to you and talk about the process of trying to work out what a word means • Facilitate paired and small group discussion so children are able to reflect and learn together	• Emphasise the different paths to word learning • Encourage children to ask when they do not know a word • Celebrate word learning achievements regularly
Images and objects	• Use images and objects to support word learning where possible. This may be an image on the Word Wall or use of artefacts in history, for instance	• Explicitly link the image to the word meaning, particularly if abstract • Use multiple images to portray words' meanings • Provide extra opportunities for hands on experience with objects
Repetition and review	• Use the new words lots of times • Put in place review mechanisms such as the Word Pot (see page 41)	• More repetitions: children with word learning needs need to hear new words more times. This can be enhanced with songs or raps (see pages 80–82)
Teach strategies	• Build up a repertoire of word learning skills over time	• Know which strategies children need extra support with • Specifically guide the application of new strategies until used independently
Into speech and writing	• Provide opportunities for children to use the words in talk and also written tasks	• Provide extra structure, for instance sentence stems, words and images on tables, peer models and talk before writing
Have fun	• Regularly play word games • Show your enjoyment of words	• Explicitly teach games first so the vulnerable word learners can master the game before they need to focus on challenging vocabulary as well • Play games that include words that children know, just to enjoy words

Action	Good practice	Extra support in the classroom for vulnerable word learners
Link with families	• Provide opportunities for families to get involved	• Specifically reach out and engage with families of vulnerable word learners • Let families know how their child is being supported in school and how they can get involved. See pages 69–75 for handouts for families
Start soon and keep going	• Vocabulary is a long-term project, so include it in everything you do, every day • Start in Early Years and do not stop	• Take action as soon as a vocabulary learning needs are noticed • Do not wait for an assessment. Start with the strategies listed here straight away • It is hard to close the word gap once it has opened so interventions will need to be long term, regular and high quality to have an effect
Vocabulary is everywhere	• Build vocabulary teaching and learning activities into all aspects of the curriculum	• Focus on the most important words, so these learners do not get overwhelmed • Support with independent word learning skills also, so vocabulary is learnt across the day

Notice Children with Vocabulary Learning Needs

As outlined in Chapter 1 (page 2), children may have vocabulary learning difficulties for a number of different reasons. Rather than pondering too much on causal factors, for most children it is better just to notice and think about what can be done.

For young children or those with severe language learning needs it is easier to spot that their vocabulary development is not progressing as it should: they say very little. Once children start talking in sentences it can be harder to spot, but by looking specifically, vocabulary learning difficulties are noticeable in the classroom. Do not limit analysis of children's vocabulary to literacy, look across the whole curriculum. Compare the child to other class members and specifically look out for the areas listed below.

What to look out for

A checklist, 'Identifying a child with vocabulary needs', is given on page 64.

Supporting Children with Vocabulary Learning Needs in the Classroom

Talking: Use of more general words, particularly verbs, e.g.: 'I *got* the set of cards' instead of 'I *collected* the set of cards.'

Tendency to continue to use simpler vocabulary and not picking up technical words, even when modelled. For instance, in science, when recording observations, they persist with using 'saw' instead of 'observed', and in maths continues to only use 'take away' rather than 'minus'.

Understanding: this is challenging to detect even under close observation, but a child with vocabulary (or wider language) learning needs may have difficulty following instructions, class discussions or listening to stories. Difficulties may be more noticeable when talk is not supplemented by images. One behaviour that children with poor vocabulary **rarely** do, is to stop and ask speakers about words they do not know.

Reading: General reading difficulties may indicate underlying language learning (including vocabulary learning) needs. Difficulties with reading comprehension are often aligned with vocabulary learning so difficulties answering questions about what they have read is one sign to look out for. For fluent decoders, asking the child to explain more challenging words they have read will reveal if they are reading for meaning and again may indicate vocabulary learning needs. In group reading, does the child stop and ask about unknown words? This is a good strategy for long-term vocabulary growth, but how challenging are the words they are asking about?

Writing: as a more permanent record it is often the easiest way to spot vocabulary learning issues. In creative writing, is a child's use of vocabulary as rich and wide as expected? Are topic words that have been specifically taught apparent in a child's written work? Some children may be cautious to use words they are unsure how to spell, so writing cannot be the only measure, but it is one warning sign.

Talk to other staff members who interact with the child you are concerned about and ask them to reflect upon the above points as well. If they are at all unsure, come back to them in a week or two and see if they have had any further thoughts.

Spend a moment interacting with the child.

- Talk about a special interest they have, and when they use any specific vocabulary ask them what it means. Most hobbies come laden with specific vocabulary, so if they do not use any, then this is also an indication.

- Read a story together and stop to discuss any mildly challenging vocabulary.

- Review a piece of written work and prompt them to verbally 'upgrade' the vocabulary used.

- Discuss a recent topic and first just notice the use of specific vocabulary and then also ask them to define key words.

- Talk to them about what they do when they encounter a word they do not know.

Speak to families as well. The home environment makes far fewer demands on vocabulary, so quite often families of children with vocabulary difficulties (even when severe) do not have concerns. Asking questions such as these may draw out more specific information:

- what was the last word you were surprised that your child could use? (typical vocabulary development is very rapid at times and families notice it), and

- Does your child ever ask you about words? Can you think of a recent example?

If the home language is not English, then these questions relate to the home language.

If you suspect the child has severe needs with vocabulary or has wider language and learning needs, you are advised to seek specialist advice.

Have a Plan for Supporting Children with Vocabulary Learning Needs

As outlined in Chapter 1 (page 2), vocabulary learning needs are common and their impact is significant, so all schools should have a plan for supporting these children. It may not be needed all of the time, but it should be ready as and when required. Staff either need to be trained or have easy access to training.

Adults do not learn all of their words from one source, and neither do children. Additionally, vocabulary reflect all aspects of learning and life experiences, so it makes sense to build a team that involves everyone who works with and knows the identified children. That includes families, teachers, teaching assistants and Special Educational Needs Co-ordinators (SENCOs). Everyone has a role to play as words need to be heard multiple times in different contexts and we all use them differently, but equally validly. By working together, we can provide optimal word learning opportunities.

The average English speaker knows an estimated 30,000 to 50,000 words, and so working out where a child's word learning gaps are can take a very long time, especially as it is so specific to the individual. A detailed assessment is needed for children with severe difficulties and is best conducted by a specialist. For most children it is better to have a general idea, start supporting their vocabulary and fine-tune it as you progress. Assessment tools are provided in Chapter 3 (page 32).

Focus on the Classroom

As written earlier, the focus of the support plan should be the classroom. High-quality vocabulary instruction this will support all word learners. For those with additional learning needs it is easy to add in extra if it is all working well in class. Trying to supplement poor classroom practice with an intervention is likely to be unsuccessful.

An out of class group (or individual) intervention that has a curriculum focus has a number of advantages. The words are going to be used in class and so without any extra effort children will be exposed to the words many times. The reverse is that children will also have a reason to use the words, as they talk to peers, explain their thinking or complete written work. Curriculum- related words are gateways to learning, thus improving children's ability to engage with content. Children can see the immediate impact that word learning has. They are not just learning random words, they are learning words that their peers are learning, and words that allow them to understand and talk about what is happening in the classroom. This all boosts engagement and self-image as a word learner.

Teach Important Words: Quick Overview of Process

The word gap between those with additional needs and their typically developing peers can be daunting. It is unrealistic to expect any intervention to close this gap. Instead we can focus on words that matter; the words that impact most on learning. By teaching specific curriculum words we can minimise the impact of word learning difficulties and increase access to the curriculum. For this reason, *Word Aware 3* focuses on content areas of the curriculum such as mathematics, science and history, rather than English/literacy. The rich vocabulary of English/literacy is obviously important too, but it is generally more accessible (if taught well) and individual words generally have less impact on learning. More is written about teaching words from literacy on page 26.

For direct teaching of vocabulary, *Word Aware* uses the STAR approach, which stems from Blachowicz and Fisher's (2015) work. STAR stands for 'select, teach, activate and review'.

Select: There is limited teaching time, so word selection is crucial. The selected words should be at the right level and important to the curriculum, so they directly impact on learning.

Teach: The process used in the classroom and in the group are the same. It is designed to be quick and simple. The aim is to start the word learning process in the group so that full understanding can naturally develop as children encounter the word over time. In effect, the teach process is about highlighting which words are important and kickstarting the word learning process rather than teaching the word completely. The group children take the word into class and because they have a small head start, they are better able to access the whole class teaching and develop a full understanding.

Activate: During the activate stage, children have the opportunity to bring the new word to life. To fully know a word, children need to be able to integrate the new word with their existing knowledge and understanding of the world. This is done by making explicit links to how the word applies to them. For instance, the word **prototype** can be activated by having discussions whilst the children build **prototypes** of products which they have designed. The children hear the new word in context, so they are building up a fuller understanding of the word. After learning the word **habitat,** the children then learn about rabbits' **habitats** and deepen their knowledge of **habitats**.

Review: This is the final part of the process. The purpose is for children to encounter the target words again, in spoken or written form, thus continuing their learning. If children do not encounter words again, the risk is that they are forgotten. The pace and episodic nature of much of the curriculum presents obstacles, as the focus moves to the next topic and associated new words rather than looking back and embedding previous teaching. Our maxim is 'if it's worth doing, it's worth reviewing'. If words have been selected, taught and activated, it is crucial that they are then reviewed.

Teaching Important Words: In Depth

Selecting words

The first letter in STAR stands for 'select'.

Word Aware uses the following classification for words. This is completed by the class teacher reflecting upon the whole class's vocabulary knowledge for a specific topic. It can be used in any curriculum area that has specific vocabulary to be learnt such as mathematics, science, history or geography. Start with a list of words that children need to access the subject area and then sort according to the criteria outlined below. There is no national standard, but with practice teachers can complete it reliably and quickly. It can be used with any curriculum.

Anchor words	Goldilocks words Not too easy and not too hard, but just right	Step on words
Children have a thorough understanding of these words. Everyday spoken and written language for a child of this age. Used at home and in daily interactions. Children may have become familiar with this vocabulary through prior teaching.	**Really useful words** Likely to be encountered again in reading or oral language. Average adult has a **good** level of knowledge of the word. Words that are very topic specific but are core to the topic. Age 7+: Desirable for children to use in their writing.	Less likely to be encountered again in reading or oral language. Average adult does **not have much** knowledge of the word. Words that are particularly topic-specific and are not core to the topic. Age 7+: Not a word that children usually need to use in their own writing.

Supporting Children with Vocabulary Learning Needs in the Classroom

'Goldilocks' words are the words that are selected to be taught to the whole class. A judgement needs to be made about children's level of vocabulary. If unsure, then ask the children to quickly rate their knowledge and define a few of the words. It may be that some children with vocabulary learning needs do not know some 'Anchor' words. In many topics it will not be possible to teach all of the words that children do not know, so select the ones that will have the most impact on learning.

If at all possible, focus on 'Goldilocks' words, but if children do not know key 'Anchor' words, then these will need to be prioritised for the group. If a child regularly does not know lots of the 'Anchor' words, then individual advice should be sought from a specialist. For children who do not know most 'Anchor' words, the approach outlined in this book may still be used, but it will need tailoring to their individual needs.

A blank copy of the 'Whole class vocabulary planning sheet' is available on page 67.

Examples of Anchor, Goldilocks and Step On Words

Subject	Age group	Topic	Anchor	Goldilocks	Step on
Geography	6–7 years	Weather	*spring* *summer* *autumn* *winter* *hot* *cold* *windy* *snow* *weather*	*climate* *drought* *flood* *seasons* *temperature*	*forecast* *precipitation* *warm front* *water vapour*
Science	6–7 years	Uses of everyday materials	*bendy* *card* *cardboard* *changed* *pull* *push* *glass* *twist* *weak* *strong* *squeeze* *squash* *see through*	*absorbent* *elastic (v)* *flexible* *material* *property* *fabric* *waterproof* *un/suitable* *rigid* *transparent*	*opaque* *translucent* *reflective* *hessian* *polyester*

Subject	Age group	Topic	Anchor	Goldilocks	Step on
Mathematics	8–9 years	Fractions (including decimals)	*part* *equal parts* *fraction* *one whole* *half* *quarter* *third* *tenth*	*eighth* *sixth* *fifth* *twentieth* *proportion* *decimal point* *decimal place* *equivalent* *rounding* *convert*	*decimal fraction* *proper fractions* *improper fractions* *recurring*
Design and Technology	9–10 years	Sliders and levers	*control* *move* *push* *pull* *in a line* *round*	*pivot* *input* *lever* *linear* *mechanism* *process*	*linkage* *bell crank* *cam* *reciprocating* *oscillating* *rotary* *slider*
Science	10–11 years	Evolution and inheritance	*fossil* *vary* *environment* *identical* *characteristics*	*adaptation/ adapted* *offspring* *suited/suitable* *variation* *evolve* *extinct*	*genes* *chromosomes* *hereditary* *natural selection*

Liverpool School Improvement (2018), English National Curriculum (2013) and National Centre for Literacy and Numeracy (1999)

Teaching words

The 'T' in STAR stands for 'teach'.

The main focus of the group intervention is to pre-teach words to children that they will be exposed to in class. The group will provide children with greater opportunities for repetition and lay the foundations for learning more about the word. The group members will have a clear understanding that they can then develop naturally as they learn more in the classroom. The group gives children a boost that allows them to access learning.

Key features of pre-teaching are that it should be timed to coincide with the class teaching as closely as possible. Ideally on the same day, but if not then the day before. The group should allow for children to hear the word many times. The word should also be defined using very simple words and sentences that the children understand. There should be opportunities for children to learn about how the word relates to them. Where possible, objects should be used, but only when they add meaning.

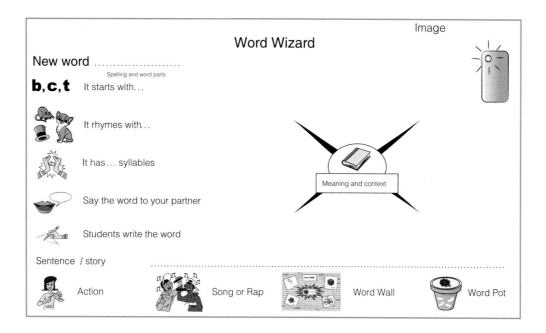

The word then needs to be explicitly taken from the group into the classroom. This facilitates the learning being generalised beyond the group.

In both the group and in class the 'teach' process is based around the 'Word Wizard', a small illustration of which is above, and full details of which are provided in the next chapter (page 32). Phonological (speech sound) and semantic (meaning) features of the selected word are identified and presented systematically on the 'Word Wizard'. Clear definitions and links to the children's experiences are provided. Multi-sensory experiences, including images, actions and songs are added to enable the child to remember the word. Once you are confident with using the 'Word Wizard', it should take no longer than five minutes to teach a word.

As part of the process the word (accompanied by the image) is placed on the Word Wall. This is a *working* Word Wall, and words go up and are interacted with. It gives the new word a profile and reminds children and adults which words they are learning.

The other word learning tool is the Word Pot. Details of how to make a Word Pot are on page 83. This is critical, as it is how words are brought from the class to the group and back. Words learnt in the group (and in class) are placed in the Word Pot and taken out and discussed from time to time.

Teaching Goldilocks words in class: these are the words that the whole class will be learning about. If the word taught in the group is a Goldilocks word, it is straightforward, as group children will have a head start on their classmates, and when the teacher asks 'who knows about this new word?' the group members will be able to respond positively. The group members can then learn alongside their peers and grow their knowledge of the word.

Anchor words: these are the words that most children in the class already know. They are still related to the topic and so will be encountered but will not have the profile of their Goldilocks counterparts, as they will not be taught to the whole class. They still need to be taken into class, but extra opportunities to learn about the word need to be engineered. The class teacher will be aware of the word, as it has been brought into class, but it might be about completing an abbreviated teaching sequence with the whole class or just with the group children.

Activate

The 'A' in STAR stands for 'activate'.

By this point in the process children have a partial understanding of the word. The activate phase is when children deepen their understanding of the new word. To do this effectively they need to hear the word being used meaningfully. This is why selecting curriculum-related words is so important as the activate phase is most effective when it is within the rich language context of the classroom. The words that are being taught will be used by teachers and other children as they learn about the topic. The natural word learning process will happen, with little planning or additional effort. This can of course be supplemented by structuring learning, so the word is encountered more times, e.g.: if the target word is **categorise**, then children need to experience sorting toys as well as foods and rock types.

Activation can be enhanced by asking reflective questions that require children to re-think their knowledge of the word, create new links and deepen understanding. Questions such as 'what does **reasonable** mean?' do not require deep thinking whereas 'would you think it was **reasonable** if I asked you to read the whole book for homework tonight? Why or why not?' requires much deeper processing. A further example for **categorise** that requires deeper thinking is: 'What things do you **categorise** at home? And why?'

To access this type of activation question children must have well-developed language skills, so simpler tasks such as forced choices, e.g.: which one of these is **absorbent**, the swimming trunks or the goggles. Images will support learning.

If the word that has been taught in the group is a 'Goldilocks' word, then whole class activate tasks can be used. If the group word is an 'Anchor' word, it will still be linked to the lesson, so the same practical tasks should still apply, but this will need to be supplemented by teaching staff doing the following:

- Ensure the word is visible on the Word Wall and highlight this to the children;
- Continue to use simple terms to define the words, as well as simple synonyms. If not direct synonyms, then explain the differences;
- Model use of the target word in different contexts as much as possible so that the children hear it many times and learn more about the word from hearing its natural use;
- Continue to give examples of how the word relates to the children's lives as well as the topic being studied; and
- Encourage students to use the new word. Provide feedback on their efforts.

Review

The final part of STAR is 'R' for 'review'.

Review activities should happen in both the classroom and the group. Working Word Walls and Word Pots need to be part of the routine, but you can also use the ideas provided or any of your own. Review activities need to provide meaningful encounters with the words. Much better to have a 30-second discussion about when and where children experienced 'decaying' leaves rather than send them off to find the letters 'd-e-c-a-y-i-n-g' in a word search.

Children with vocabulary learning needs have greater difficulty with learning words, but they also have issues with retaining them. They need to encounter words that they have previously learnt more frequently than their typically developing peers. Reviewing words needs to be a standard part of classroom practice, so Word Walls and Word Pots should be established and regularly used. Reviewing words is built into the group structure, but families can get involved also. This is all outlined in Chapter 3 (page 32). In the classroom, children with vocabulary learning needs can be prompted to do independent review activities, such as reviewing words recorded in their own word book, making a 'fortune teller' (see page 128) or playing games such as 'Shaboo' (see page 127) with peers.

Full details for whole class teaching of topic vocabulary are provided in *Word Aware 1*, 2nd edition (Parsons & Branagan, 2022). Details of the group teaching of vocabulary are outlined in Chapter 3 (page 32)

'Slippery' Words

There are some words which are more challenging to learn than others. We have coined the term 'slippery' words because they are hard to learn and keep hold of. These slippery words are abstract concepts which are often challenging to gain an understanding of through hands on learning. Examples of slippery words: 'criteria', 'attributes', 'relationship' and 'ecosystem'. And because hands-on learning is not always possible, they need to be explained by words. This of course makes them particularly slippery for our children with vocabulary learning needs. Unfortunately, these words abound within the curriculum and so cannot be avoided.

Before you teach any 'slippery' words, it is important that you plan carefully. The following steps will help all children, but particularly those with language learning needs.

For the teach phase:

- Make sure you fully understand the word's meaning and how it relates to this topic. Look it up in the dictionary or glossary and talk to a knowledgeable colleague;

- Have a very clear and simple definition. Make sure it captures the meaning accurately. Check the children know any words that you use in your definition; and

- Avoid using opposites or other words that might be confused unless these words are very well-known by all of the children.

For the activate phase, use a combination of:

- Hands-on learning: practical tasks which directly show the word's meaning;
- If hands-on learning is not possible, then provide infographics or short videos. Again, make sure these show the meaning and are not distracting;
- Provide a range of different examples;
- Support connections to what children already know; and
- Support children to use the new term. Model how to use it, but also prompt them to use the word in context, e.g.: 'talk about caterpillars using **life cycle**'.

Top tip: For children aged 9 to 15 years, focusing on science vocabulary, Lift Lessons provide communication-friendly videos to support understanding of key concepts: www.liftlessons.co.

These words may take extra time, but it is worth spending extra time to ensure they are well established. Once a simple, clear foundation of the word is formed it can then be built upon (activated) in the classroom. Without a strong foundation, learning opportunities in the classroom cannot be utilised.

Linking Class, Group and Home

The words are sourced from the whole class curriculum, established in the group and then the learning is built upon in richer, more natural settings. This can be the classroom, but it can also be the home environment. After all, we want children to be using the words across their whole lives.

Engage families in the process and explain how they can get involved. Families will have different capacities, so adjust the demands accordingly. Family involvement should not be onerous. It should be enjoyable and an opportunity for child-led conversations that really support the child in working out how the new words fit in their world. The key message is 'talk to your child about these words' so it does not require extra resources, just a few minutes once in a while. Families are welcome to do more, and further guidance is provided on pages 69–75.

The key message for families with English as an additional language/English language learners is to support vocabulary learning in the home language. This can make the home–school relationship slightly more complex, but it is crucial for vocabulary growth and long-term bilingualism.

Literacy-related Words

The approach outlined in this book is focused on curriculum-related words from subjects such as mathematics, science and history. This is because only a small number of words can effectively be taught, and these words are the key to accessing the curriculum. They are also more 'conceptual' and linked to new ideas and so more challenging to learn.

This does not mean that the rich vocabulary sourced from books is not important. It is extremely important. To read more challenging books and to write effectively children need a wide vocabulary. Sourcing and teaching words from books is a key component of *Word Aware 1*, 2nd edition (Parsons & Branagan, 2022). The approach recommends ad hoc identification of Goldilocks words from shared books. This eliminates a need for detailed planning, but also prevents pre-teaching, as outlined in this book. The literate vocabulary sourced from books will quite frequently be synonyms of words children know. This makes them easier to learn, provided a simple synonym can be identified. The challenge with many of these words is when and how to use them. If not taught well, children may make direct swaps for synonyms, for instance using 'stared' instead of 'glance'.

Extra Strategies to Support Vulnerable Word Learners

Children with additional vocabulary learning needs can be supported in the classroom by adding a few extra strategies into the whole class teaching.

- They need to hear the word <u>more</u> times, and have the phonological (speech sound) elements emphasised more;

- Have <u>more</u> opportunities to hear the word used naturally;

- Link the new word back to a simple word that they are familiar with. Make this link explicit and when one word would be used and not the other. This can be recorded in a drawing or written down;

- Act out ways of walking, moving and speaking;

- Use images. Look for several examples and non-examples of adjectives and compare;

- Record the word in a personal dictionary; and

- Write the word in examples sentences or a mind map.

Building a Vocabulary Team

Children do not learn all their words from one person. They need a team of people. The following table provides a quick guide to roles and responsibilities. Photocopy this page and the following one and give to all involved, so everyone knows who is doing what. Further details and resources for each role are provided in Chapters 3 and 4.

Everyone has a role to play with teaching children new words. Focus on the classroom, as that is where lots of important words are needed, but supplement this with focused small group work and brief home activities. Have fun, celebrate success and talk to each other to check how things are going.

Person	Role
Special educational needs coordinator (or equivalent)	• Coordinates who attends the group • Sets up the training for all staff • Ensures the group facilitator knows who to go to when there are issues • Liaises with the class teacher about timetabling the group • Ensures the group facilitator has time to prepare resources • Ensures assessments/monitoring are happening at relevant intervals (see page 57)

Person	Role
Group facilitator	• Participates in training • Prepares resources for the group (many of which may also be used in class) • Runs the group twice per week • Follows the group guidelines • Liaises with the class teacher about the words and materials • After each group facilitates the children taking the word back into class • Fills out weekly attendance sheet (page 132) • Conducts assessments/monitoring as directed • Reports back on progress and raises issues
Class teacher	• Participates in training • Identifies key words to be taught in the group • Provides simple definitions of these words to the group facilitator • Directly teaches the whole class Goldilocks words • Ensures taught words are displayed on the class Word Wall and in the Word Pot • Uses the target words and encourages children to use them also • Models use of 'word detective' strategies and relates this back to the 'word detective' bookmark • Fills out 'teacher feedback' form (page 133)
Teaching assistants in class (who may also be the group facilitator)	• Is aware of the words that have been taught in the group • Uses the target words and encourages children to use them also • Ensures the 'word detective' bookmark is available and prompts child to use at appropriate times • Praises children when they use any of the target words
Families	• Put the 'Fridge words' on your refrigerator or noticeboard (page 68). Talk about these words where possible. Use these words in sentences, telling your child more about what these words mean • Celebrate success as your child is going to come home with certificates • Play word games (see pages 69–73) and just have fun enjoying words • Occasionally talk about not knowing words and show your child how you look them up on your phone or ask someone else • Look at non-fiction books which relate to the same topic. This will provide more opportunities to talk about the new words • Read to your child or encourage them to read and/or listen to audiobooks. This is good for general vocabulary growth. • Information sheets for families are on pages 74 and 75.

Staff Training

Staff training is outlined in Chapter 5. The slides and a video presentation are available via the companion website that accompanies this book. The presentation gives an explanation of the principles and practicalities of the group. It is **essential** that group facilitators, class teachers and anyone supporting them, watch this training. It takes approximately one and a half hours.

FAQ for Planning

As a class teacher I find it hard knowing which words the group children will and will not know.

It is hard to predict for every child. Plan for the whole class and sort into 'Anchor'/'Goldilocks'/'Step on'. Ask one or two children of the group children what they know about a few of the anchor words. This will give you a rough guide. Choose 'Goldilocks' words if you can. Do **not** use 'Step on' words to focus on in the group.

Some children know the words that are being taught.

It is highly likely that at some point words will be selected that some children in the group know. This is OK once in a while. If this is happening regularly to the same child/children, then either their inclusion in the group or the level of words needs changing.

Is it better to focus on one subject across the year or try and cover them all?

This probably comes down to individual judgement. Where is the extra support going to have the most impact? It might be that students need support with mathematical vocabulary. Or it might be about focusing on 'slippery' words, which are abstract, harder to learn at the speed of the whole class, but which impact on learning.

Topic words are not being selected and taught in class.

If this is due to a temporary issue such as staff absence or whole class teaching is planned to start shortly, then hold on for a few weeks. Whilst you wait, in the group focus on word learning strategies and playing games with the aim of just enjoying words. If this is an ongoing issue, then the group facilitator should speak to the Special Educational Needs Co-ordinator. If the issue cannot be resolved, then the group should be put on hold until direct teaching of curriculum words is established.

Words are not categorised as Anchor/Goldilocks/Step on.

As above it is OK for a couple of weeks, but action should be taken if the issue continues and the group paused until such a time as the curriculum words are able to be provided.

Is this group suitable for children who are learning English as an Additional Language (EAL)/English Language Learners (ELL)?

For typically developing EAL/ELL children who are very new to English then this group may provide an opportunity with focused English conversation. It would be anticipated that these children would progress quickly. EAL/ELL children may have issues in their first language, just as monolingual children do. These children will benefit from the group, but additional home language activities will need to be included so families can get involved.

Some children do not know any of the anchor words.

If it is several children, it could be that the words are not being categorised accurately. Check if others in the class know them. If it is just one or two children, then advice from Speech and Language Therapists/ Speech-Language Pathologists or specialist teachers should be sought.

We only have time for one group per week.

Time in schools is pressured, but once a week only allows for the teaching of about 30 words per year. Even if children learn all of the words it will have a limited impact. There is also less opportunity for reviewing words. Better to run two very short groups and truncate the activities. You will need to do more in class to compensate.

Is this group suitable for one-to-one sessions?

Yes. A group is ideal as children can learn from each other but if there are no others in the class who need support then the activities all work with individuals.

References

Blachowicz, C. & Fisher, P. (2015). *Teaching Vocabulary in All Classrooms*, 5th edition. New York: Pearson.

Liverpool School Improvement Service (2018). *Making Words Work*. Liverpool.

National Centre for Literacy and Numeracy (1999). *Mathematical Vocabulary*. Reading.

Parsons, S. & Branagan, A. (2022). *Word Aware 1: Teaching Vocabulary Across the Day, Across the Curriculum*, 2nd edition. Abingdon, Oxon: Routledge.

Web-based resources

English National Curriculum (2013) www.gov.uk/government/collections/national-curriculum (accessed 1 June 2021).

Lift lessons www.liftlessons.co (accessed 1 June 2021).

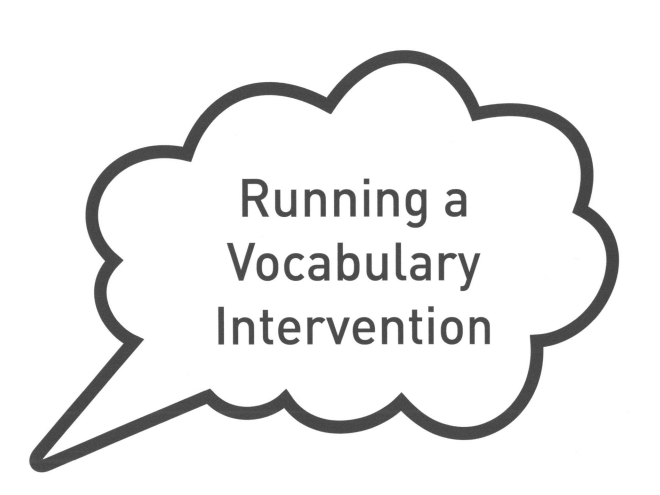

Running a
Vocabulary
Intervention

Chapter 3. Running a Vocabulary Intervention

If children attend a group where they learn words and they receive no further support for vocabulary learning they are unlikely to make significant progress. Vulnerable word learners need access to:

- Whole class teaching of vocabulary (see Chapter 2 and *Word Aware 1*, 2nd edition, Parsons & Branagan, 2022) and

- Extra strategies to support vulnerable word learners (see page 27), in addition to

- Small group teaching and support at home and in class.

This chapter focuses on the last part: small group teaching and support at home and in class.

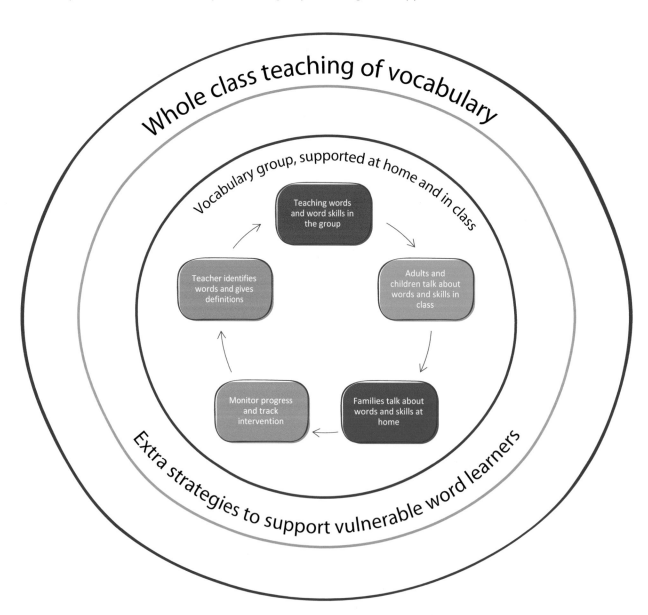

Planning for a Vocabulary Group

Chapter 2 provides guidance about identifying children for the group. This page outlines the practicalities of setting up the group.

Who

Three to five children per group is optimal. The group members will all need to be in classes which share the same curriculum because the words being targeted in the group will be closely linked to what is being taught in class.

When

Groups should be run twice per week for approximately 20–30 minutes. The taught word should be introduced in the group BEFORE the word is taught in class. This gives the group children a boost, so that they can learn rather than be overwhelmed by the whole class teaching.

Planning

For this intervention to be effective it needs a close partnership between the group facilitator and the class teacher. The class teacher is responsible for identifying the words that are going to be taught in the small group. The words can come from any curriculum area but must be linked to what is being taught in class. The teacher used the 'Whole class vocabulary planning sheet' (page 67) to identify key words to teach. The teacher also writes a simple definition that all the children will be able to understand. These words are written on the 'Fridge Words' sheet provided on page 68. This is then used by the group facilitator to enable effective and accurate teaching of the word. It will also be sent home to families.

Preparation

Before the group is commenced, the group facilitator should spend some time organising all the resources that are needed. Once this has been done, very little preparation time is needed. The resources are in Chapter 4. The only additional items required that are not provided in this book are:

- A plastic spinner for the 'Word spinner' activity (page 118)
- A pot with a lid to make a Word Pot (to hold pieces of paper with the target word written on them) see page 83. This should generally be kept in the class and just be borrowed for the group session.
- A blindfold for the 'Blindfold game'.

> **The teacher identifies words and gives definitions**

The group must not be an 'add on', working in isolation. It is a part of the learning process and so the words taught in the group <u>must</u> be linked to what is being taught in the classroom. So, it is the class teacher who is responsible for selecting the words that will be taught and reviewed in the group. Chapter 2 provides specific guidance on identifying the words to be taught (page 20).

> **Teaching words and word skills in the group**

There are two parts to the intervention:

1. Teaching and reviewing identified words
2. Developing word learning skills.

The first five sessions use the same structure, which includes introducing a new word and developing word learning skills. The sixth session then recaps the words that have been taught in the previous five sessions.

Sessions 1–5	Introduce a word per session
	Plus developing word learning skills
Session 6	Review all five words taught in the previous five sessions

This cycle is then repeated with a new set of words.

Group Structure (Introducing New Words)

Display the visual timetable of activities. These are given on page 76. Refer to the pictures as you start each activity.

Fridge Words 	Before the first session write all five words on the 'Fridge Words' sheet on page 68 and send it home.
	During each session remind children that the words are on their fridge at home. Encourage children to talk about the words with other family members.
Warm-up word game 	Play a general word game: 'Thinking Hat', 'word associations', 'I went shopping', 'Letter sound and category', 'I give you this gift', 'Word rounds' or 'Dictionary definitions'. Details are provided on pages 37–39.
	The purpose is to focus group members on words and enjoy words but also develop word learning skills informally.
Learn a word 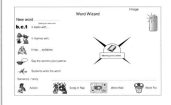	Teach the word using the Word Wizard (page 79). Full details are provided on page 41.
	This activity builds up the word bit by bit, focusing on each element of the word, so it is established on a strong foundation. It is also a chance to practise identifying the speech sounds (phonology) in words.
	Group members write the word in their individual word books.
Word learning skills	Pick one of the 'Word learning skills' activities. Do one activity per session. Details are on page 44.
	We want all children to be independent word learners. Children with word learning needs often need to be taught these skills in smaller steps than their peers.

Board game 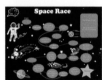	• Choose a board game to play, e.g. 'Word Spinner', 'Space Race', 'Beetle'. See pages 118–125. • Review the word taught today and the word taught in the previous session Words need to be heard and seen again to be learnt, but also retained.
Connect the group and class	Children need to make connections with the word learnt in the group and the learning in the class. It is crucial to support this otherwise the learning may stay in the group. Use the sheet 'Linking the words to class, What shall we do today?' (see page 126) to choose a way of taking the word into class. Here is an example: Give the new word to the class teacher. Put it on the class Word Wall.

Sessions 1 to 5: Teaching New Words

Families talk about words and skills at home

Fridge Words

Send the five new words home written on the 'Fridge Words' sheet (page 68) and encourage families to place them on their refrigerator at home and talk about the words. Encourage as much engagement as possible by sending home a fridge magnet, or a colourful pin for a noticeboard for families with integrated whitegoods. Encourage families to take photos of their Fridge Words so that words can be talked about at a later date. Ask children to talk about sentences their families used.

- Talk to parents, asking them to use the words in a sentence or tell their child about the word. Children need to hear the words used naturally in sentences. Parents should avoid asking their child too many questions as children will have limited knowledge about the new words. If family members are not sure what the words mean, then they can look up the words in an online dictionary.

- Remember, at home they can talk about these words in any language. Where possible translate the words and sentences into each family's home language.

- At the end of each session remind children that these words are on their fridge (or encourage them to make sure the sheet is on their fridge).

> At home, all conversations about words should be in the language that **parents** are most fluent in. Learning the word in the child's home language will support English vocabulary learning.

Warm-up word games

Word games are used at the start of each group to focus the children on learning about words as well as building their word learning skills. They are intended to be played with simple, familiar words. Choose one game per intervention session. They should only take a minute or two.

The games can easily be played with the whole class. Encourage children to play them at home as well. Invite families into school and children can teach family members the games.

Thinking Hat	A variation on 'I spy', except the word does not need to be visible and word-meaning clues are given rather than letter sounds. Say, 'I put on my thinking hat and think of something that is (give a clue).' If incorrect say, 'It's not that. I put on my thinking hat and think of something that is (original clue and a second clue).' Continue until the word has been guessed. If children have difficulty thinking of words, then use pictures which are hidden from others' views.
Word associations	One player starts by saying a word. Any familiar word will do. The next player says a word that is related to the first word. It can be related in any way. If another player cannot see how the words are related, they can challenge, and the connection needs to be explained. Keep going until a word is repeated or a connection cannot be explained. Here is an example: Egypt – Mummy – Dad – beard – Santa Claus – Christmas – trees – leaves – Autumn. Opportunities to discuss words with multiple meanings often arise.
I went shopping	One person starts by saying, 'I went shopping and I bought a …' (names a food item). The second player says, 'I went shopping and I bought …' and repeats the first player's item before adding their own. The third player continues saying the first two items before adding their own, and so on. See how many items group members can remember. Variation: 'I went on holiday and I packed…' or 'I went to the (place) and saw…'
Letter sound and category	A letter sound and a category are chosen by different group members. Make sure the letter is said as a speech sound (phoneme). Players then take turns thinking of items that belong in the category that begin with that speech sound. For instance, a food beginning with 'ch': cheese, chocolate, chips … Categories with lots of examples: Food, animals, verbs (doing words), adjectives (describing words), boys'/girls' names, places. Go around the group once or set a timer and see how many the group can think of collectively.

I give you this gift	This activity targets adjectives. Before you start you will need a feely bag and some interesting objects. As a group, think about the ways in which objects can be described. For instance, it might be by colour, size, texture or a specific attribute. One child chooses an object from the feely bag. This child gives it to the next child using the phrase, 'I give you this (name the object) because it is (adjective).' The sentence describes the object, for example, 'because it is shiny', or 'because it goes fast'. (From Nash, 2013)
Word rounds	Choose a category; use the word round category cards given on page 77. Then go around in the group naming items in the chosen category, e.g. something with legs: 'chair', 'person', 'table', 'cat', 'ladybird'.
Dictionary definitions	Use an appropriately accessible dictionary such as the Collins COBUILD Learner's Dictionary (2018) or a picture dictionary. Choose one child to say a letter of the alphabet. The adult then finds a page in the dictionary with that letter. Then choose another child to select a number between one and ten, e.g. seven. The adult then counts down the page until they get to the seventh word. Without saying the word, the adult then reads the definition or describes the picture. The children know the initial letter and meaning, so their task is to guess the word.

Sessions 1 to 5

Learn a Word

In advance

- Print out the Word Wizard (page 79).

- Have the completed 'Fridge Words' sheet (page 68) to hand (with the identified words and simple definitions).

- Each word needs an image. Options for images:

  o A quick hand drawing

  o 'Communication in Print', widgit.com (cost)

  o 'Boardmaker', myboardmaker.com (cost)

  o The 'create' option in Twinkl, twinkl.co.uk/create. This is free but has limited symbols

  o ARASACC, arasaac.org. This is also free but with limited symbols.

  o Search for images online.

- Print off one of the songs or the Word Rap on pages 80–82. There are also sing-along versions available on YouTube. Search for 'Word Aware songs'.

- Before the first session, agree with the class teacher the location of the Word Wall in the classroom. The Word Wall is for all children. It should be at child height to allow children to interact with it. After each session the words will need to go on the Word Wall in the classroom. Words are added as they are learnt. This reminds both children and adults to think and talk about these words in the classroom.

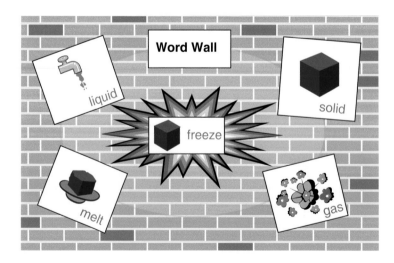

- Make sure the class has a Word Pot (a plastic pot with a lid. You write words on a piece of paper and put them in the pot). See page 83 for 'How to make a Word Pot'. You will need to borrow the Word Pot for each group session (and then return it).

- Print off the 'Rate your word knowledge' on page 84.

- Provide a word book and a pencil for each child. This can be a standard small notebook but it should move between the class and the group.

In the group

Introduce the word

- Ask the group to rate their knowledge of the new word. Use the 'Rate your word knowledge' on page 84.

- Write the new word on a Word Wizard sheet. The example below is **nutrients**.

- Underline any spelling patterns.

- Draw a line through the word to indicate prefix (beginning), base and suffix (end) if applicable

e.g.: new word:

settlement

For **nutrients** highlight 's' makes it a plural. If children are familiar with 'nutrition', then briefly highlight 'nutri'.

- Present the image or symbol. Attach the symbol or quickly draw a picture on the Word Wizard sheet. Briefly talk about what how the image relates to the word, especially if the link is not obvious.

Speech sounds and writing

- Ask the children to all say the first speech sound (phoneme) in the word. It is important that this is the speech sound rather than the letter. For the **nutrients** example, write 'n' on the Word Wizard.

- Ask each child to think of a word that rhymes with **nutrients**. Any word, real or nonsense, will do, e.g.: lutrients, sutrients, putrients. Add these to the Word Wizard.

- Instruct all group members to say the word and clap the syllables of **nutrients**. Clap three times as you say 'nutrients'. Add '3' to the Word Wizard.

- Instruct the children to say the word to the person sitting next to them.

- Instruct the children to write down the word in their own word book (any small notebook). Dependent on time and literacy abilities you may also ask them to add further information about the word's meaning later in the group.

Meaning

- Ask the children if they know anything about the word. Record <u>accurate</u> contributions on the Word Wizard sheet. For the **nutrients** example, one child may say 'fruit'. Add this to the Word Wizard. For words that have more than one meaning, focus on one meaning at a time.

- Read the simple definition from the lesson plan and use this to add key words to the Word Wizard sheet, e.g.: '**Nutrients** help animals and plants grow.'

- Talk about the word and how you use it. Talk about which lesson and topic it relates to, and also how it relates to children's lives, e.g.: 'To grow strong and healthy we need different **nutrients**.'

- As a group, generate a sentence that shows something of the meaning. You may start off with a generic sentence such as 'You need lots of **nutrients**', so extend this by asking 'why?' to prompt a more meaningful answer such as 'to make you strong and healthy'.

Action, Rap, Word Wall and Word Pot

- Make up an action for the word. An action for **nutrients** could be miming eating and thumbs up (to indicate good food). Do the action and say the word at the same time.

- Use the 'Word Rap', 'Word Song' or 'Spell it out song' on pages 80–82. Follow the instructions, e.g. using the Word Rap 'Say the word **nutrients**, clap the word **nutrients**, read the word **nutrients**, act the word **nutrients**, shout the word **nutrients**, whisper the word **nutrients**.' With the songs and the rap, insert the new word so that the children say the word many times. There are also some sing-along versions on YouTube. Search for 'Word Aware songs'.

- Write the word on a piece of paper and add it to the Word Pot. This is the class Word Pot which is borrowed just for the duration of the group and will be returned to class with the children.

- Directly after the group session is finished, ask a child to take the word and put it on the Working Word Wall in the classroom. At a suitable time, the class teacher can also acknowledge the new word and discuss it with the group or whole class.

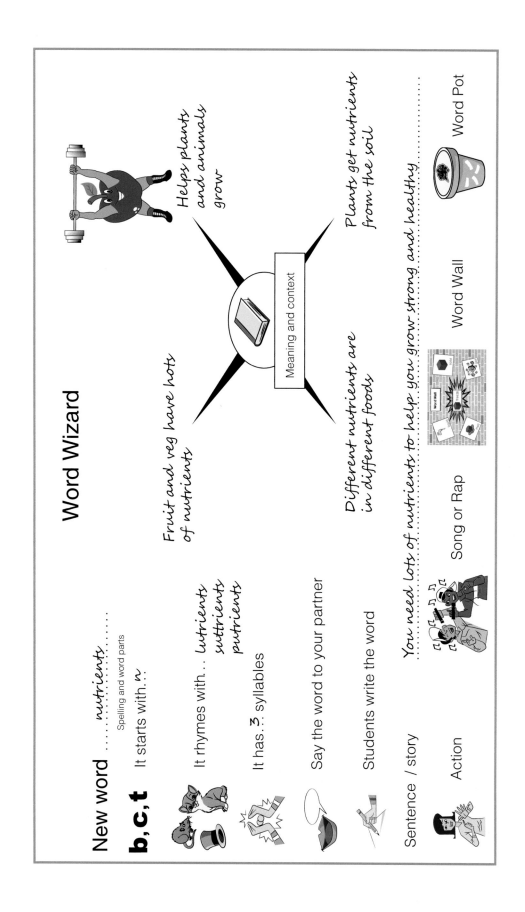

Sessions 1 to 5

Word Learning Skills

You can either work through each activity in order or pick a particular area to focus on, based on assessment (see Assessment of Word Learning skills on pages 135–137). The activities may also be used with the whole class, but group members are likely to require more opportunities to embed the learning than their typically developing peers.

Choose one activity per session as this is only one part of the intervention. Each separate activity is given in a row below. Activities may need to be repeated in other sessions, sometimes several times.

Although assessed in the 'Assessment of Word Learning Skills' (pages 135–137), there are no specific activities provided for developing awareness of speech sounds in words, as this is covered when implementing the Word Wizard activities.

Compound words	Copy the words on pages 85–86 (only do one page at a time). Cut out these words. Mix them up. Instruct children to match two words together to make a new word. Support if children have difficulties with reading. It is possible to use some of the words more than once. Talk about the 'small' words and the compound words and what they mean. Take turns to use the 'small' words and compound words in sentences. Use drawings to emphasise meanings.
	Further compound words are available via the companion website which accompanies this book.
	Look at the sentences on page 87. Encourage the children to spot words that are made up of two shorter words (compound words).
	Look at the paragraphs on page 88. Instruct the children to spot words that are made up of two shorter words (compound words).
Looking at the ends of words (suffixes)	Print and cut out the 'Words to add endings to' and 'Word endings' cards on page 89. Take in turns adding word endings to change the words. Read them out before and after the ending is added. Use the word with and without the word ending in sentences. Discuss how the ending changes the word. This is a spoken task and does not need to be written, but there is the option to write the words and sentences should you wish to.
Looking at the beginning of words (prefixes)	Cut out the words on page 92 ('Words starting with "un"') and page 94 (When "un" means "not"). Look at the words together and read them out if children struggle. Look within words for any parts of the word that children recognise (e.g. well, tie, kind). Talk about how 'un' changes the word. Refer to 'What does "un" mean?'. There a couple of examples where there is an 'un' at the start, but it doesn't mean 'not'. 'Uncle' and 'united' are just words that share the same spelling pattern. These should also be discussed. Take it in turns to make up sentences containing the words which start with 'un' meaning 'not'. This activity can be completed orally, but you may add a written component should you wish.

	Repeat the above using 're'. The resources are on page 93.
	Cut out the words on page 92 ('Words starting with "un"') and page 94 (When "un" means "not"). Give each child a pair of scissors and instruct them to cut off the 'un' prefix. Talk about how the prefix changes the word. Make up sentences with the words with and without 'un'. Talk about the words that have 'un' at the start but not as a prefix. The examples are 'uncle' and 'united'. Do not cut the 'un' off these words.
	Repeat the above using 're'. The resources are on page 93.
	Look in a dictionary and collate further examples of words beginning with the target prefix. Write them down highlighting 'un' or 're'. Discuss non-examples such as 'read'.
	Give each child half a piece of A4 card. Each child then folds the card in half. They then write 'un: means "not"' on the front. Then on the inside of the folded card they write as many words starting with 'un' (that mean not) as they can. Set a challenge for the children to collect more words as they listen or read. The same activity can also be completed for 're'.
	Further prefix resources for the prefixes 'dis', 'non', 'mis', 'il', 'im' and 'ir' that are not in the book are available via the companion website which accompanies this book.
Multiple meanings	Cut out the words on page 95. Take turns to pick a card. Between you, think about what the different meanings are. You can talk about it, act it out or draw the meanings. Do as many as you have time for.
	Print out the sentences on page 96. In each sentence identify a word that has more than one meaning. Discuss which meaning is the right one. Encourage children to talk about what helped them work it out.
Applying word learning skills	Print out the bookmark on page 97. Give one to each group member. Reflect on each skill and allow the children to tick each one to indicate it has been covered.
	Copy page 98 and read one sentence at a time together. Use the bookmark as a prompt to look for compound words, prefixes, suffixes and words with multiple meanings. Circle or underline parts of words that fit the criteria. Discuss the learning as the children progress. As children learn the skill, reduce the support. The aim is for the children to be able to do this independently.

	Repeat the above exercise using the paragraph on pages 99 to 101, accompanied by the bookmark on page 97. The aim is for children to develop independence so introduce the activity clearly but then provide the least amount of prompting. Support reading as required. If children are struggling with applying word learning skills, practise with sentences again.
	Photocopy a page from a book that the children are reading in class. Select it carefully so it includes a number of opportunities for prefixes, suffixes and compound words. Repeat the exercise above. Give the children the bookmark to take into class as a reminder to look within words.
Definition skills	**What am I?** Print out the 'What am I?' prompts on page 102. Print and cut up the noun cards on pages 103–106. Place in a pile upside down. A child takes a card and describes it using the prompts: You find me … I can … An important thing about me is … When you look at me, you can see … Examples: 'You find me in the kitchen. I can cook food. An important thing about me is that I get hot. When you look at me, you can see a handle and lid. I am a …' 'You find me in space. I can spin. An important thing about me is that it is the place that we all live. When you look at me you see lots of land and lots of sea.' Once the item has been guessed, discuss any additional clues that might have helped.
	Use the noun cards on pages 103–106. Print out the 'What can it do? What can you do with it?' card on page 115. **What can it do? What can you do with it?**  Each group member takes a card in turn and acts out what they can do with that object or what it can do. Once others have guessed the action, they must then guess the object. The original player then puts the word into a sentence with the verb to describe what they were acting out, e.g.: for 'keyboard', 'I was typing my homework on a computer keyboard.'

Definition skills *cont'd*	Print and cut up the verb cards on pages 107–109 and place in a pile face down. Print out the 'Clues for verbs' card on page 116.

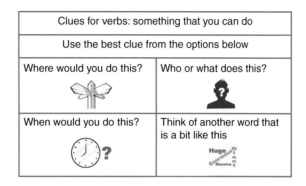

Model how to use the clue card several times. Take turns in turning over the verb cards and talking about them using the prompts. Talk about which clue was the most helpful clue.

Print and cut up the adjective cards on pages 110–112 and place in a pile face down. Print out the 'It can be used to describe … and…' card on page 116

Model how to use the clue card several times. Take turns in turning over the adjective and thinking of at least two things you can describe using this word. Others may offer suggestions.

Print out and cut out a mixture of verbs and adjectives pages 107–112. Mix them up and place them in a pile face down. Print out the 'Think of another word that is a bit like this' (page 116)

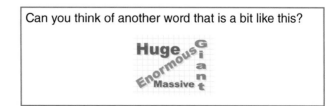

Model how to use the clue card several times. Group members then take it in turns to pick up a card and think of a synonym of the word.

Definition skills *cont'd*	Print out the noun cards on pages 103–106 and place in a pile face down. Print out the 'Clues for nouns' (page 115) and the 'Clues for any word' (page 117). Model how to use the clue cards several times.
	One child picks a card. They then choose the prompts which help them define the word best. The other group members must wait until the child has finished giving all the clues they can. To add a competitive element points may be awarded for each clue provided,
	e.g. 'ambulance': 'You can drive this, it has a flashing light, you find it on the roads or at a hospital, if you are very sick you might use this, a special thing about it is that it can make a loud noise.'
	This would get five points. As you tally the points, point to the relevant clue that the child chose, e.g.: 'you can drive; this is telling us what you can do with it, one point'.
	Only give points for helpful clues. Saying an ambulance has 'black bits' (talking about the tyres) is not helpful so would not score a point.
	If a description could fit under two clues, then just give a point for one, e.g.: a flashing light on an ambulance could be 'what can you see on it?' or 'what is important about the word?'; this would only score one point.

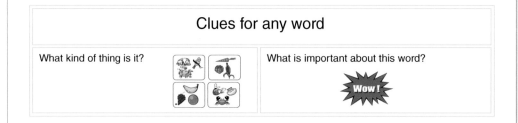

Repeat the above exercise for either verbs or adjectives, printing out the appropriate clues to match. See pages 107–112 and 116–117.

Board Games

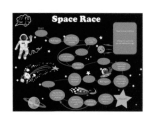

- Each game focuses on two words: today's word and the one you taught in the previous session. If you are in the first session, then include a word from the last batch of five words you taught. The game 'Take off' reviews three words so this is best done later in the block of sessions, when you have taught three words.

- It is helpful if you present the written word accompanied by a symbol, picture or real object.

- When playing these games, encourage the children to say their answers in sentences that include the target word if possible. For instance, '**nutrients** are in food'.

- Adults should take turns, as well as children, to model the expected answers.

Word Spinner	**To prepare Word Spinner** • You will need a plastic spinner to attach to the Word Spinner board provided on page 118. Spinners can be bought cheaply. Search for 'plastic arrow spinners'. • Print off and laminate the Word Spinner board on page 118 or see the companion website which accompanies this book for a printable colour version. • Fix a spinner in the middle of the circle. • Identify the two words to teach: today's word and the one you taught in the previous session. **To play Word Spinner** • Start with the word you have taught today. The children take turns to spin and carry out the relevant instruction about the target word, e.g. 'Clap the word **nutrients.**' Once all have had a turn, change the word to one you learnt previously.
Space Race, Treasure Hunt, Under the Sea, Learn a Word	**To prepare** • Print off and laminate the chosen board. They are on pages 119–122 or downloadable from the companion website which accompanies this book. • You will need the target words written on card, a die, and one counter for each player, including the group facilitator.

Space Race, Treasure Hunt, Under the Sea, Learn a Word cont'd	**To play** • Place the target word on the space indicated on the board. Players take turns to roll the die. Follow the instructions on the board. If there is a challenge, e.g.: 'Use the word in a sentence', the player must use the target word, e.g.: 'I saw **pebbles** on the beach.' The adult should take turns and join in by answering challenges about the word. The winner is the first player to reach the end. Change the word at some point during each game so adequate time to talk about the second word is provided.
Beetle	**To prepare Beetle** • Print and laminate a copy of a beetle picture and 'beetle game instructions' (provided pages 123–124). • You will need: a blank piece of paper and pen or pencil for each child as well as a die. • Place the target word in the square 'place the new word here'
	To play Beetle • Each player takes turns to roll the die. • Every time a player rolls a number that allows them to draw, they need to complete the task outlined in the table on page 124. So, if they roll a '6' they can draw the body and say the first sound of the target word. • A '6' (for body) must be rolled before anything else can be drawn. • A '5' (for head) must be rolled before the eyes and antennae can be drawn. • Continue until one player has completed their beetle. • If it takes too long for the time you have available, set the number of rolls per player and continue in another session with new words.
Take Off	**To prepare Take Off** • Print off and laminate the 'Take Off' board (page 125). • You will need three target words, each written on a card. Use the word taught today and the two from the previous sessions. Also needed are a die, and one counter for each player, including the adult.
	To play Take Off • Each player takes turns to roll the die and follows the instructions on the board. • Warning: some players find waiting to roll a '6' frustrating.

Sessions 1 to 5

Linking Words to Class

> Adults and children talk about words and skills in class

It is essential that children hear and use the new words in class and at home. A little extra thought and effort can have a big impact.

This can be facilitated by the class teacher and group leader liaising regularly. Small actions can really assist the transfer of learning to the class. Choose one or more of the activities on page 126. If you would prefer, this can be set ahead of time and a consistent process established.

Linking the words to the class
What shall we do today?

Give the new word to the class teacher. Put it on the class Word Wall.	We will add the word into the class Word Pot.
We will go into class and tell the **class** about the word we have been learning.	Listen out for the word in class. Your teacher and other adults will use the word.
We will go into class and tell the **teacher** about the word we have been learning.	We will go and show the class the Word Wizard we did today. We can teach the class the action.

Whichever actions you take, make sure you have a mutually agreed system to support children to use the new words in the classroom.

Session 6: Group Structure: Review Session

The purpose of the sixth session is to review all five words that have been taught in the previous five sessions. Make sure that each word has an equal amount of focus across the different games.

Lay out the visual timetable of activities. These are given on page 76. Refer to the pictures as you start each activity. Make sure you have all five words, each with an image.

Activity	Instructions
What am I, 1,2,3? 1,2,3?	Present each word in turn and name them. Spread the words out on the table, face up. The adult gives three clues for a chosen (secret) word. Children may guess only after all three clues are given. Talk about the clues which helped the most. Repeat for all words.
Choice of games	Choose two to three games or as many as you have time for. Ensure your choices allow for lots of opportunities to talk about the target words. 1. Act out the word 2. Pass the picture 3. Test the teacher 4. Shaboo 5. Fortune teller 6. Draw a meaning 7. Blindfold game Instructions are given on page 53.
Self Rating Scale UNDERSTANDING WORDS	Present the 'Rate your word knowledge' (see page 84). Briefly discuss each word in turn and ask children to rate their own word knowledge. Reflect on how their knowledge has changed and how they can keep their knowledge growing.
Make your own certificate Well done!	Print out copies of the certificates from the choice on pages 129–131. One for each child. Children write the words that they have learnt into the space available. Send home and celebrate.

Review Group Games

Act out the word	Place all the words and symbols face down in a pile. Group members take in turns, one at a time without showing others. The task is to act out the word, without speaking, for the other group members to guess. Discuss what action gave the greatest clues.
Pass the picture	Choose one word that has been taught. Pass around the symbol with the written word, face up. Each child is encouraged to say one thing about the word. Use the 'Word Wizard' for support if required. When the picture comes back to the original group member they summarise the most relevant information in a sentence. E.g.: '"Famine" is when there is no food to eat, because it has not rained. People starve in a famine.' Repeat for each word.
Test the teacher	Each child takes a word and hides it from view. Children take in turns to say three things about the word for the group leader to guess. They may use the completed (or blank) 'Word Wizard' for support. Talk about the clues which helped the most.
Draw a meaning	Give each child a blank piece of paper and pencils. They each select a word and write it on the piece of the paper. The aim is then to show the word's meaning by drawing a picture. Prior to drawing, have a discussion about the word, using the completed 'Word Wizard' for support if required. Discourage simply copying the symbol that has been used and encourage their own views. The drawings may then be collated into a book and used for reviewing at a later point. Another version of 'draw a meaning' is to fold the paper to make 'books' and write the word on the front page and a add a drawing inside. For both versions writing about the meaning may also be added.

Shaboo  **Don't Say It** Read the word on the card silently. Without saying the word on the card, define the word to help others guess the correct word.	**To prepare Shaboo** Adapted from: http://hubpages.com/education/Fun-Game-to-Learn-and-Practice-High-Level-or-ESL-Vocabulary-Words • Print three copies of the Shaboo cards on page 127. Cut up and laminate. Place in a box or tub (the 'instructions pot'). • You will need a die and paper and pen (to keep score)
	To play Shaboo • Place words to review on the table face down. One child takes a word to review and also a Shaboo card from the instructions pot. • Without showing the word to others they follow the instructions on the card. • Once the word has been guessed or they have successfully used the word, the player rolls the die and this number is added to the score. That is unless they get the 'lose all points' card • This can be played in teams or as a whole group. If played as a group, see if you can increase the score you got last time or see if you can score over a target number in five minutes.
Fortune teller	**To prepare the fortune teller** • Print out the blank template on page 128. • Fold as per instructions. If unsure search online for 'how to fold a fortune teller'. • Each child writes four words they wish to review on the outside squares.
	To play with the fortune teller • A 'guest' chooses one of the words. The 'owner' of the fortune teller open and closes it as they spell out the word. • Next, the 'guest' chooses one of the numbers visible. The 'owner' of the fortune teller open and closes it the corresponding number of times. • Next, the 'guest' chooses another number. The 'owner' of the fortune teller opens that flap and reads it aloud. The 'guest' must carry out the instruction as it relates to the target word that was chosen at the very start.
Blindfold game 	Place the review words face down on the table. One child wears a blindfold (or turns away). One word is turned over. Without saying the target word all other group members say one thing about the word. One player then summarises what has been said. Only when everyone has finished, can the blindfolded child guess. Repeat for all group members.

Group word map	Children work in pairs or as a whole group. In the latter the adult may act as the scribe. Write the word in the middle of the page. Similar to a mind map, information about the word is written around it. If completed in pairs, then compare each group's work. Discuss which information is most important.
Word Storm	Adult acts as scribe. Write the word on a white-board. Children call out information about the word and this is written on the board. Discuss which information is most relevant. A photo may be taken and kept as a record as well as reviewing learning in the future. ('Word Storm' term from St John and Vance, 2014).

Families talk about words and skills at home

At the beginning of the six sessions, send the Fridge Words worksheet home. Ensure families are aware of what to do with the words.

After each block of six sessions, celebrate achievements with families. Send home certificates that children have created (pages 129–131). Supplement this with 'word learner' stickers, sending home a message or a photo.

If a fortune teller has been made, this may be played at home.

Word learning skills activities such as compound words or prefix and suffix may be sent home occasionally.

Monitor progress and track intervention

It is essential that the group facilitator fills out an attendance and intervention record. This is used as a record not only of who attended, but which words were taught and what areas of word learning skills were covered. The sixth session is a review session and does not introduce any new teaching, as it reviews the last five words taught. Here is an example. A blank 'Attendance and intervention record' is on page 132.

Attendance and Intervention Record

	Week 1		Week 2		Week 3	
Words introduced	Word: carbohydrates	Word: nutrients	Word: digestion	Word: protein	Word: evidence	Review last 5 words
Word learning skills	☑ Compound words ☐ Looking at the beginning of words ☐ Applying word learning skills ☐ Looking at the ends of words ☐ Multiple meanings ☐ Definition skills					
Children	Date: 12.1.22	Date: 14.1.22	Date: 19.1.22	Date: 21.1.22	Date: 26.1.22	Date: 28.1.22
Wayne	✓	✓	✓	✓	✓	✓
Chantelle	✓	✗	✓	✓	✓	✗
Mohammed	✓	✓	✓	✓	✓	✓
Charlie	✓	✓	✓	✗	✓	✓

Monitoring Progress

The effectiveness of interventions needs to be monitored, but this needs to be balanced against the time delivering the intervention. There is no point spending time measuring an intervention's impact when little time has been spent actively working with children.

1. Evidence of using words and skills in the classroom

If the children are starting to use the words in the classroom, either saying the words or using them in in their writing, then this can be used as evidence that the group is making a difference and no specific assessment is necessary. The same goes if the child is talking about and applying word learning skills.

Use the 'Teacher Feedback' (page 133) to gather evidence from the class teacher. The group facilitator needs to fill in the first two boxes stating which words have been taught and what word learning skills have been focused on. They also add the children's names. It is recommended that feedback be collected three times per year.

2. Assessment of word knowledge

- Pick one set of five words you intend to teach.
- Assess the children just before those words are taught. Repeat the process again after the teaching and review of all five words is complete.
- This assessment process should be completed three times a year. **Do not try and assess knowledge of every word you teach**.

In advance

- Print the 'Rate your word knowledge' given on page 84.

- Print 'Assessment of word knowledge' sheet (a blank form is on page 134) for each child. Write the five words that are going to be taught, onto this sheet.

When working individually with each child

- Ask the child to rate their knowledge of each word in turn by pointing to the 'emoji indicators': 'I don't know it', 'Not sure' or 'I know what it means' on the 'Rate your word knowledge' (page 84).
- Tick the relevant box on the 'Assessment of word knowledge' on page 134.

- If the child says that they know the word, then encourage them to 'tell me what you know about this word'. Record their answer on the form. If the child gives an answer which only gives partial information (a score of one), encourage them to 'use the word in a sentence'. Mark (SP) to indicate 'sentence prompt was used'. Use of this prompt limits the maximum score to two. A score of three is given when a child can define a word, not just use it appropriately in a sentence.

- For words with more than one meaning: if a child defines the wrong word meaning, then encourage them to think of another meaning that applies to this topic. If they cannot define the relevant meaning, the score is 0.

Afterwards

- Score the answer using the scoring criteria below. It is sometimes necessary to discuss children's definitions with a colleague. Scoring examples are provided on page 143.

Scoring Criteria

Never heard of it or has heard of it but unable to provide any further relevant information. Score 0 if the child can define another meaning of the word but not the one targeted here.	0
Gives some information about the word but it is missing important points.	1
Most key information provided, but some points left out, so may still be a bit general or mildly confusing. If they cannot fully explain the word but can use it in a sentence, then the maximum score is 2.	2
Clear definition and unlikely to be confused with another word.	3

3. Assessment of word learning skills

The assessment of word learning skills looks at all the basic skills that are covered in the word learning skills section in the group.

- Compound words
- Looking at the ends of words (suffixes)
- Looking at the beginning of words (prefixes)
- Multiple meanings
- Applying word learning skills
- Definition skills

It also focuses on speech sounds in words (phonology). These skills are frequently repeated during teaching of the word using the Word Wizard.

Print out the 'Assessment of word learning' on pages 135–137 and copy one per child. Then print one set of the 'Assessment of word learning resources' on pages 138–140. Cut out the outside of each box. Words that are attached together, should stay together.

Follow the instructions on the assessment.

Interpreting the assessment

Add the scores up. It is suggested that the lowest scoring area becomes the focus for intervention, but practitioners may have reason for starting with another skill area. For instance, it might fit more closely with what is being taught in class. Each section of the assessment corresponds with a word learning skills task. The exception to this is 'speech sounds in words' (phonology). If this is an area for development, then extra emphasis should be put on these tasks when teaching new words. Phonological tasks will be repeated for all new words so there are plenty of opportunities for practising these skills.

If a child is able to accurately complete all of this assessment, then more focus needs to be placed on using the skills when looking at sentences and in using these skills in the classroom.

Assessment of Word Knowledge

| Child's name Wayne Smith | Year group 3 | Date 5.1.2022 |

☑ **Before** Intervention   ☐ **After** Intervention

| Words | Child self-assessment | | | If the child says they know the encourage them to 'tell me what you know about this word.' If they give an answer which only gives partial information (a score of 1), say, 'use the word in a sentence.' Mark (SP) to mean 'sentence prompt was used'. Write what the child says here. | Score |
	Never heard of it	Heard of it but not sure what it means	Knows what it means		
Carbohydrate			✓	Not really sure.	0/3
nutrients		✓		-	0/3
Digestion			✓	Eating. (SP) When you eat your food is digestion in your tummy.	2/3
Protein	✓			-	0/3
Evidence			✓	When you find something. (SP) I saw some evidence.	1/3

Total score: 2/15

Scoring criteria

Never heard of it or has heard of it but unable to provide any further relevant information. Score 0 if the child can define another meaning of the word but not the one targeted here.	0
Gives some information about the word but it is missing important points.	1
Most key information provided, but some points left out, so may still be a bit general or mildly confusing. If they cannot fully explain the word but can use it in a sentence, then the maximum score is 2.	2
Clear definition and unlikely to be confused with another word.	3

Troubleshooting

Skills needed to access the group

To be able to access this group effectively, children need to be able to participate in simple conversations with adults and peers about topics they have not chosen and to be able to talk a little about words' meanings when asked.

What to do if a child is not making progress

By coming to a group, a child is missing teaching time in the classroom, so the intervention needs to be effective. If a child is not making progress, then the first thing to do is stop and reflect on the reasons. Are the words at the right level? Do they have the prerequisite skills outlined above? Are they able to engage with the activities? Are there any support activities and strategies happening in the classroom or at home?

Small changes to the teaching style and content can sometimes have a big impact. It is helpful to talk to someone, and ideally the other person should observe the group. It may be necessary to call in outside help.

What to do if a child knows a word

The children in the group will all know different words, and from time to time it is likely that they will know some of the words already. This is OK if it is occasional, as they will deepen their understanding and gain confidence with known words. If it gets to the point where a child knows most of the words, consideration should be given to their group membership. If most of the children know a word before the intervention, then a new word should be selected.

What if all the children know the word?

If you start teaching a word and it is obvious that all the children know the word, go on to the next word on the list. If you have no more words, then just review the words you have recently taught.

The children do not know some of the words used in the definition

Think of simpler terms to define the word. If this is not possible, then use hands-on activities to show the meaning. Feed this back to the class teacher.

Listening and attention

Many children need support to focus their attention. Make sure you keep praising them when they are showing good listening behaviours. Picture symbols are widely available. When children are doing what you want them to do: tell them If a child is not doing what you want, use this as a prompt to comment on another child who is doing the right thing. Effective rules are:

- Looking at the person who is talking
- Sitting still
- Staying quiet
- Listening to all the words.

(Spooner & Woodcock, 2019)

References

Collins COBUILD Primary Learner's Dictionary (2018). Glasgow: HarperCollins.

Nash, S. (2013). *Communication and Language Activities.* Buckingham: Hinton House.

Parsons, S. & Branagan, A. (2022). *Word Aware 1: Teaching Vocabulary Across the Day, Across the Curriculum,* 2nd edition. Abingdon, Oxon: Routledge.

Spooner, L. & Woodcock, J. (2019). *Teaching Children to Listen in Primary Schools: A Practical Approach.* London: Bloomsbury.

St John, P. & Vance, M. (2014). Evaluation of a principled approach to vocabulary learning in mainstream classes. *Child Language Teaching and Therapy,* 30:3, 255–271.

Chapter 4. Intervention Resources

Identifying a Child with Vocabulary Needs

Please refer to page 17 for further information and interpretation.

Child's name: **Date:**

General observations

	Observations
Using general vocabulary • Does the child tend to use more general words, particularly verbs? e.g.: 'I *got* the set of cards' instead of 'I *collected* the set of cards.'	
Using topic-specific vocabulary • Does the child tend to continue to use simpler vocabulary and not pick up technical words, even when modelled? e.g. 'saw' instead of 'observed', 'take away' rather than 'minus'.	
Understanding vocabulary • Does the child have difficulties following instructions, class discussions or listening to stories?	
Reading • Can the child answer questions about what they have read? • Can the child explain some mildly challenging words they have read? • In group reading, does the child stop and ask about unknown words? How challenging are the words they ask about?	
Writing • In creative writing, is a child's use of vocabulary as rich and wide as expected? • Are topic words that have been specifically taught apparent in a child's written work?	

Finding out more: working with a child

Task	Observation prompts	Observations
Talk to the child about a special interest they have. When they use any specific vocabulary ask them what it means.	• Do they use a range of specific words? • Do they know what the words mean?	
Read a story together and stop and discuss some (mildly challenging) words you might expect a child of this age to know.	• Do they understand a range of different words?	
Review a piece of the child's written work and prompt them to verbally 'upgrade' their vocabulary.	• Are they able to think of a range of better words to use?	
Discuss a recent class topic and first just notice the use of specific vocabulary and then also ask them to define key words.	• Does the child use the new vocabulary that has been introduced in the topic? • Can the child explain topic words that have been previously taught?	
Ask them about what they do when they encounter a word they do not know.	• Do they have any strategies to work out or find out what a word means?	

Talking with the child's family

What was the last word you were surprised that your child could use?	
Does your child ever ask you about words? Can you think of a recent example?	

If the home language is not English, then these questions relate to the home language.

If you suspect the child has severe needs with vocabulary or has wider language and learning needs, you are advised to seek specialist advice.

Whole Class Vocabulary Planning Sheet

Year group:	Subject:	Topic:
Anchor words	**Goldilocks words** Not too easy and not too hard, but just right	**Step on words**
Children have a thorough understanding of these words. Everyday spoken and written language for a child of this age. Used at home and in daily interactions. Children may have become familiar with this vocabulary through prior teaching.	**Really useful words** Likely to be encountered again in reading or oral language. Average adult has a **good** level of knowledge of the word. Words that are very topic-specific but are core to the topic. Age 7+: Desirable for children to use in their writing.	Less likely to be encountered again in reading or oral language. Average adult does **not have much** knowledge of the word. Words that are particularly topic-specific and are not core to the topic. Age 7+: Not a word that children usually need to use in their own writing.

Fridge Words

Your child has been learning these new words in school. Please put this sheet on your fridge or noticeboard to remind your child which words they have been learning. Talk to them about the words. Talk about the words rather than ask too many questions. Show your child how you use the words. Take turns with your child to use these words in sentences.

Please stick this on your fridge

Word	Definition

REVIEWING WORDS

For Families: Play Word Games at Home

In school your child will be learning lots about words and you can get involved in that too. One simple way to do that is to play word games. Word games are fun, but they also help children to learn important word learning skills. Play them whenever you have a moment. It can even be when you are travelling somewhere: walking home, in cars, on buses or trains. You just need to have learnt a couple of games, so you are ready to play at any time. The first few games are the easiest.

I went shopping

This game is good for developing memory. One person starts by saying, 'I went shopping and I bought a …' (names a food item). The second player says, 'I went shopping and I bought …' and repeats the first player's item before adding their own. The third player continues, saying the first two items before adding their own. And so on. See how many you can remember. A variation of this game is: 'I went on holiday and I packed …'

What am I?

For younger children, riddles need to be straightforward, rather than the conundrums that older children enjoy so much. Three to four simple clues are usually adequate, for example:

- You find me …
- I can …
- An important thing about me is …
- When you look at me, you can see …

Example: 'You find me in the kitchen. I can cook food. An important thing about me is that I get hot. When you look at me, you can see a handle and lid. I am a …'

I spy

Play the traditional 'I spy' game. 'I spy with my little eye something beginning with … (letter)'.

Variation 1: Thinking hat. Word meaning clues are given rather than letters and the object does not need to be within sight. Say, 'I put on my thinking hat and think of

something that is (give a clue).' If incorrect say, 'It's not that. I put on my thinking hat and think of something that is (original clue and a second clue).' Continue until the word has been guessed, e.g.: 'I put on my thinking hat and think of something that is spicy.'

Variation 2: Big brain. In this game players give a clue containing the first sound of the word as well as a word meaning clue. Unlike 'I spy', players do not need to be able to see the item, but they need to think with their 'big brains'. For example, 'I think with my big brain, something that is part of a tree and begins with a "b".'

Word rounds

Choose one of the categories below. Go around the circle, with each player adding a category item.

Variation: After you have chosen your category set a timer on your phone for one minute. Taking turns around the group see how many words can be generated in one minute. Record the family total and then try to beat it next time.

Easier

Animals	Clothes	Food
Things you can see at the seaside	Things you would see at the zoo	Boy's/ girl's name
Transport	Things in a classroom	Verbs (things we can do, e.g. jump, walk, swim)

Harder

Things you can cut	Things you can smell	Toys and games
Somewhere you go on holiday	Countries	Adjectives (describing words, e.g.: short, pink, smelly)

Things that are cold	Things with legs	Sports
Things that grow	Books	Emotions
Things that are fast	Things that are red	Things that open
Furniture	Living things	Things that make noise
Shops	Breakable objects	Things that are long

What can it do?

Pick one of the words below. As a family, think of five things that it can do or that can be done with it. For example, **tree**: climb, chop, grow, fall down and absorb carbon dioxide.

apple	baby	ball	bread	chalk
giraffe	leaf	lion	lollipop stick	paper
paperclip	pencil	penguin	rubber band	stick
tree	your foot	your hand	cat	flour
flower	hair	water	air	spoon

Alison is an acrobat in Asia

Starting at the beginning of the alphabet the first player must generate a name, profession and place that all begin with that letter. For example, for the letter 'a': 'Alison is an acrobat in Asia.' The next player then has to do the letter 'b': 'Bob is a builder in Benidorm.' Make it more complex and add adjectives, so it becomes 'Alison is an ambitious acrobat in Asia.'

Describe it!

Take a look at www.pobble365.com and look at the amazing images. Choose a picture and talk about it in turn. Support your child by taking it in turns to talk about all the things you can see, how the picture makes you feel, what might someone be thinking, what might happen next, how someone or something is moving, what might someone say or what sort of person they are. Make the picture the start of an exciting adventure story.

What's the same and what's different?

Select two related words from a topic that your child is interested in and together talk about what is the same and different about the two items.

- Book or film characters, e.g. Superman and Batman, Sirius and Voldemort
- Sports, e.g. rugby and football, basketball and volleyball.
- Hobbies, e.g. different computer games, computer games and board games, reading and films
- Restaurant chains, e.g. Nandos vs McDonalds

If you want to you can draw or write them down.

Don't say it!

Cut out the words below or think of your own words. They might be related to what your child has learnt at school or any words that they are familiar with. Place all the words in a 'hat'. Each person takes a turn at taking out words from the hat. The challenge is to describe the word without using the word at all.

hill	trolley	graph	desert
dinosaur	fly swat	spaceship	cornflakes
mountain	biscuit	storm	flood
tree	umbrella	bee	baby

geography	daisy	crocodile	cinema
planets	purse	moon	present
spider	earthquake	tiger	America

Word associations

One player starts by saying a word. The next player says a word that is related to the first word. It can be related in any way. If another player cannot see how the words are related, he/she can challenge and the connection needs to be explained. Keep going until a word is repeated or a connection cannot be explained. Here's an example: Egypt – Mummy – Dad – beard – Santa Claus – Christmas – trees – leaves – departs – trains.

20 questions

One person thinks of an object. Others try and guess what it is by asking questions. The original player can only answer yes, no or maybe. Give a clue if they are on the wrong track. Can they guess it in 20 questions?

For families: Children Learn Words when They Listen to Stories

Stories are fun, but they are also a great way to learn new words which in turn will help your child in school. Stories use much richer vocabulary than we do when we talk to each other. Words from stories are also more memorable.

Keep reading to your child even if they can read well, as this will expose them to more challenging words than what they are able to read. If your child struggles with reading, then it is even more important that you read to them. Otherwise they will miss out on the rich vocabulary that comes with stories.

Get children listening to audiobooks and podcasts too, as they are another way to hear rich vocabulary.

It's great for children to listen to audiobooks on their own but it's even better to listen to them together and share your enjoyment. Long car journeys are the perfect time to share a story. Shared earphones can also work on trains or when you are waiting somewhere. Talk about what is happening. Stop once in a while and predict what might happen next. If you miss a bit, ask your child to explain. If you are at home, draw pictures of what you think characters and places might look like. Discuss similarities and differences. Act out exciting parts.

Choose a word that you heard in the audiobook. Talk about its meaning and write it down and stick it somewhere like the fridge or a noticeboard. Together with your child look up the word's meaning on your phone. Challenge everyone in the family to use it and listen out for it. At the end of the day say it in a new sentence.

Search online for 'free audiobooks' or speak to your local library about accessing audiobooks for your child. There are a number of free or cheap options.

Helping Your Child Learn Words

Learning words is really important. The more words your child knows, the more it will help them with learning.

When families help their children learn words, it really makes a difference.

It's about talking as much as reading and writing, so talk about words.

If your child comes home with a word from school or you find a new word in a book, tell them more about the word. Try not to ask them too many questions. Instead show them how you use the word.

Encourage reading for the fun of it. Read to your child, take them to libraries, find books or magazines about things that interest them or listen to audiobooks.

If you don't know a word, look it up on your phone or in a dictionary. That way you are showing your child how to learn more.

If you speak another language at home, talk about meaning of words in the language you are most confident in.

Have fun and join in!

 # Group Visual Timetable

Sessions 1–5 New words	Session 6 Reviewing words
Fridge Words	What am I, 1,2,3? _1,2,3?_
Warm-up word game 	Choice of games
Learn a word 	Rate your word knowledge
Word learning skills	Make your own certificate _Well done!_
Board game 	
Connect the group and class	

Word Rounds Categories

Animals	Clothes
Sports	Countries
Things that are long	Things that make noise
Things you can cut	Things you can smell
Things that open	Things you would see at the zoo

Things that are cold	Things with legs
Food	Transport
Things that grow	Toys and games
Verbs (doing words)	Furniture
Living things	Feelings
Things that are fast	Things in a classroom

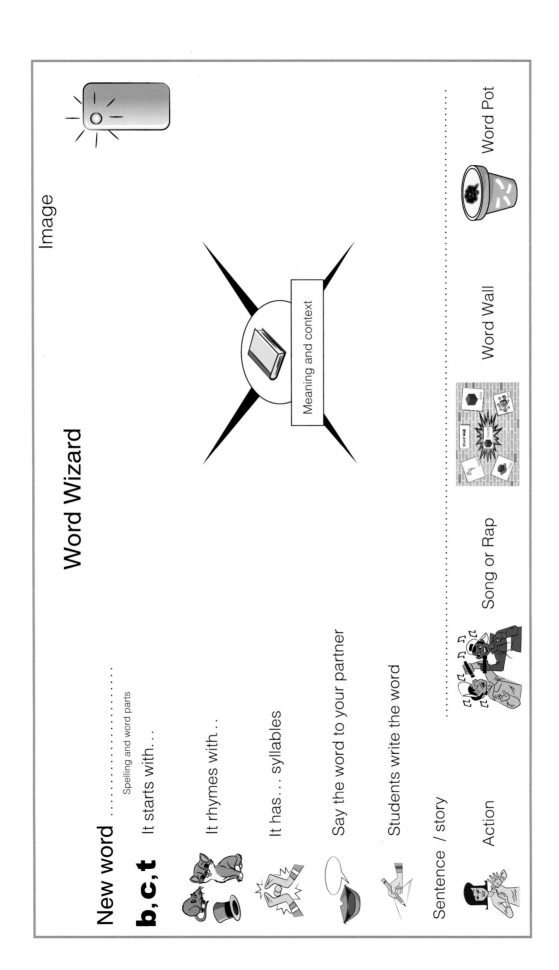

Word Wizard

Image

New word ....
Spelling and word parts

b, c, t   It starts with...

It rhymes with...

It has... syllables

Say the word to your partner

Students write the word

Meaning and context

Sentence / story

Action

Song or Rap

Word Wall

Word Pot

 WORD RAP

Say the word. . .

Clap the word. . .

Read the word. . .

Act the word. . .

Shout the word. . .

Whisper the word. . .

LEARNING WORDS

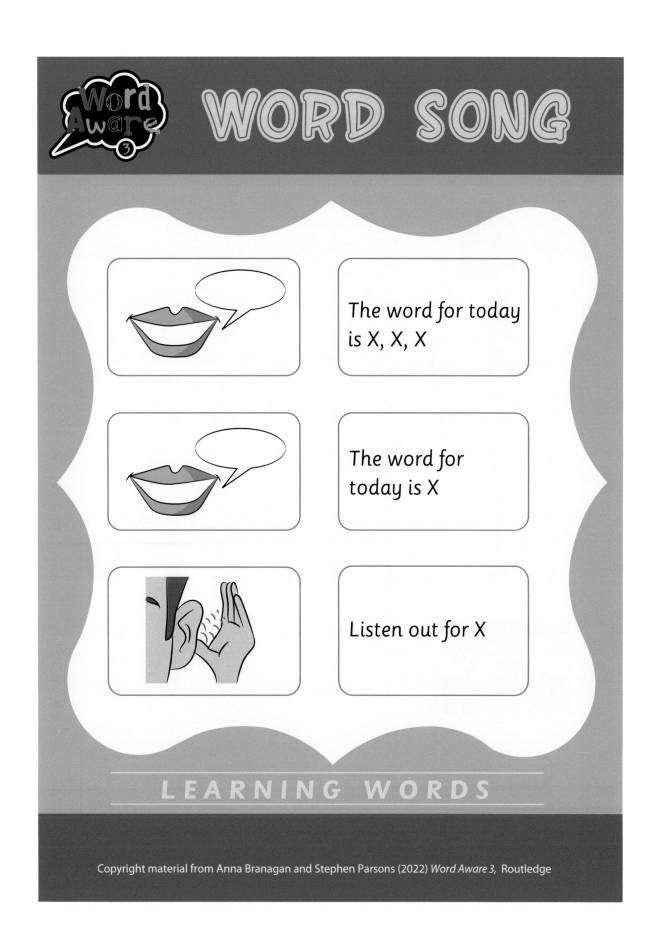

SPELL IT OUT SONG

	Give me a/an ..., Give me a/an ..., Give me a/an ..., What does it spell?
	What did you say?
	Say it again?
	Now clap it out
	And act it out
	And say it one last time

LEARNING WORDS

 ## How to Make a Word Pot

Find a container with a lid. It can be any shape, so long as it is sturdy and can be closed. Cut out the *Word Aware* symbol to go on the top of the pot. Cut out the question prompts and stick them to the sides of the pot. Both the *Word Aware* symbol and the question prompts are below and on the companion website which accompanies this book. A similar version may also be purchased in sticker format from www.language-forlearning.co.uk/shop/Foundation-Stage-and-Key-Stages-1-and-2/Vocabulary

What can it do?	What does it look like?	Describe it to someone else.
Think of something that can be described as (target word.)	Why is this an important word to know?	When might someone do this? When might you do this?
Where might you see this word?	Think of a time when you could use this word.	I like/don't like this word because ...
Which other word is a bit like this word? How is it different from that word?	Think of another word that is connected to this word. How are they connected?	How will you remember the word?

Rate Your Word Knowledge

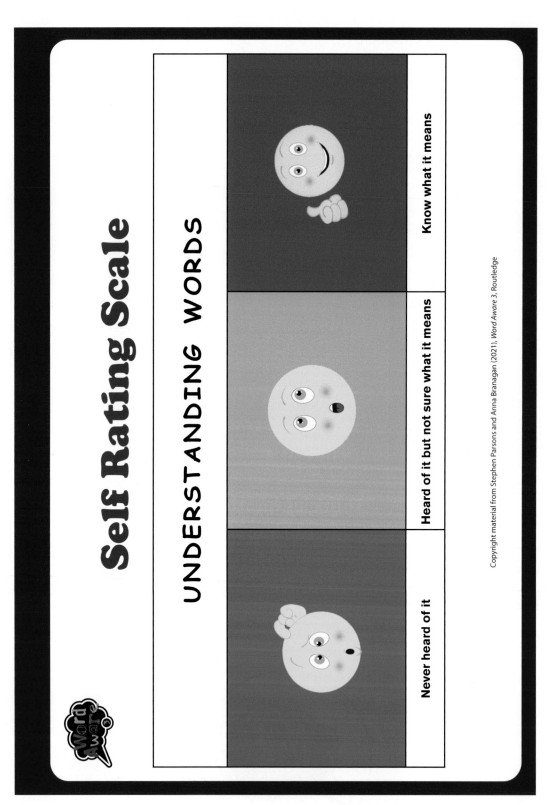

Compound Words (Two Words that Make a New Word)

bath	room
foot	ball
sun	glasses
jelly	fish
lip	stick
key	ring
down	stairs

motor	bike
round	about
water	melon
tooth	ache
play	ground
snow	ball
head	phones

From list at www.firstschoolyears.com

 Sentences with Compound Words

Children may read the sentences, or they may be read to them and discussed.

Spot any long words that are made up of two shorter words. Write or tell someone what the two short words are.

The boy had bad toothache.
The bathroom was smelly!
The snowball hit me in the face.
My mum fell off her motorbike.
I love eating watermelon.
The jellyfish swam past me in the sea.
I like to go fast on the roundabout.
She dropped toothpaste on her jumper.
We are going to the seaside.
Sunflowers can grow very tall.
We got soaked in the thunderstorm.
My favourite lipstick is red.
Your sunglasses are downstairs.
I really like eating leftovers.
The football went into next door's garden.

 ## Story with Compound Words

Children may read the paragraph, or it can be read to them and discussed.

Spot any long words that are made up of two shorter words. Write down or tell someone what the two short words are.

I think most teachers like playtime because it is when they can drink tea in the staffroom. A few teachers have fun when they are on playground duty. In our school Mr. Amir always wears sunglasses outside even when there is not much sunshine. He brings with him a special whistle on his keyring. He acts like he is a football referee blowing on his whistle. That makes everyone laugh.

Words to Add Endings To

Nouns (add 's' only)

cup	plate
phone	jumper
cow	horse

Verbs (add 'ed', 'ing' and 's')

walk	talk
pick	call
start	end
ask	jump
pull	play
help	kick
call	chew
wink	zoom
paint	add

Word endings

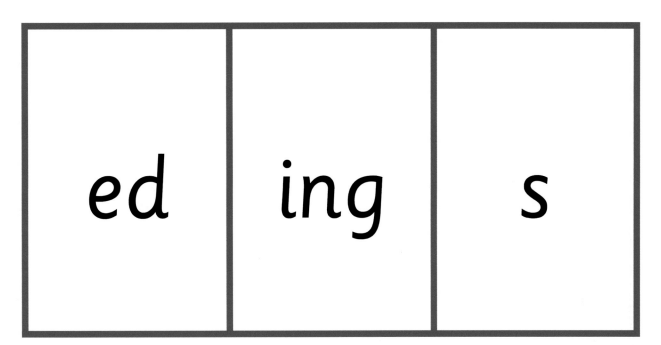

| ed | ing | s |

 Words Starting with 'un'

unfair	untie
unhappy	untidy
unwell	unfinished
unlock	unkind
unpack	untrue
unlucky	uneven
uncover	undo
uncle	united

http://www.firstschoolyears.com/literacy/word/other/prefixes/worksheets/un-%20word%20and%20definition%20cards.pdf

Words Starting with 're'

restart	refit
redo	repay
refresh	renew
repaint	refill
reread	resell
reheat	rejoin
retry	rebuild
real	restaurant

http://dictionary.kids.net.au/wordsstartingwith/Re

When 'un' Means 'Not'

'un' but it does not mean **not**

'un' means **not**

When 're' Means 'Again'

're' but it does not mean **again**

're' means **again**

Words that Have More than One Meaning

bat	letter	fly	light
chest	can	sign	park
back	right	club	box
sink	fair	lie	second
mummy	match	left	ring
bark	roll	spring	pupil

Words that Have More than One Meaning

Look at the underlined word in each sentence. It has two meanings. Talk about what it means in this sentence. What clues helped you work out the meaning? Think of another meaning for each underlined word.

The fresh <u>roll</u> smelled delicious.	_____
Jess found an old wooden <u>bat</u> in the shed.	_____
Mothers always tell their children not to <u>lie</u>.	_____
The <u>letter</u> was three pages long.	_____
He learnt to <u>box</u> at the gym.	_____
The <u>sink</u> was blocked and smelly.	_____
Femi <u>left</u> for work at eight in the morning.	_____
It was sunny, the day we held the <u>fair</u>.	_____
The <u>mummy</u> in the museum looked dusty.	_____
I felt the <u>fly</u> land on my hand.	_____
I need a <u>match</u> to light the fire.	_____

'Be a Word Detective!' Bookmarks

Be a word detective!	**Be a word detective!**	**Be a word detective!**
I can find words made up of other words, e.g. snow/ball	I can find words made up of other words, e.g. snow/ball	I can find words made up of other words, e.g. snow/ball
I can find words that start with prefixes like 'un' and 're', e.g. unfair, redo	I can find words that start with prefixes like 'un' and 're', e.g. unfair, redo	I can find words that start with prefixes like 'un' and 're,' e.g. unfair, redo
I know how the end of a word changes what it means, e.g. cat/cats, walk/walking	I know how the end of a word changes what it means, e.g. cat/cats, walk/walking	I know how the end of a word changes what it means, e.g. cat/cats, walk/walking
I look out for words that have more than one meaning, e.g. mummy	I look out for words that have more than one meaning, e.g. mummy	I look out for words that have more than one meaning, e.g. mummy

Applying Word Learning Skills

Use with the 'Be a Word Detective!' bookmark on page 97. Break it down and look for one thing at a time. Start with words made of other words and then work your way down the bookmark.

1. Pass me a match, so I can relight the fire.
2. Mummy made me rewrite the letter and sign it.
3. At the seaside we touched some jellyfish.
4. Zelda is unlocking the bathroom door.
5. I found my sunglasses as I unpacked the chest.
6. Nobody wanted to buy the recycled ring.
7. Ziggy repainted the sign untidily.
8. Dad asked if anyone wanted pancakes.
9. I feel unwell because I have a second toothache.
10. At lunchtime they were eating reheated leftovers.

Applying word learning skills paragraph 1

Use with the 'Be a Word Detective!' bookmark on page 97. Break it down and look for one thing at a time. Start with words made of other words and then work your way down the bookmark.

> The October fair was coming to town. 'You cannot go yet as your room is still untidy!' Mum shouted upstairs. 'It was so unfair!' muttered Chantelle. To make tidying her room go quicker Chantelle put in her headphones and started. At last Mum said she could go. Chantelle got into town just in time to meet her friends. They went shooting at the rifle range. Chantelle had three shots but missed. She thought she was unlucky, but nobody else wanted a rematch. Her friend Laura wanted a drink, and they found a stall that sold refills. Next, they tried the throw the ring game. Chantelle won some toy sunglasses.

Applying word learning skills paragraph 2

Use with the 'Be a Word Detective!' bookmark on page 97. Break it down and look for one thing at a time. Start with words made of other words and then work your way down the bookmark.

Josh looked out the window at the sunshine and thought about his friends playing football in the playground. He was not allowed to go yet, as he had unfinished homework.

The task was to rewrite a fairytale in his own words. Josh used his best handwriting because he knew his teacher would make him redo it all if it was messy.

Just as Josh finished his story there was a huge thunderstorm. 'Life is so unfair', Josh grumbled to himself.

Applying word learning skills paragraph 3

Use with the 'Be a Word Detective!' bookmark on page 97. Break it down and look for one thing at a time. Start with words made of other words and then work your way down the bookmark.

Even though Vanessa was only 8 years old she liked to think of herself as a top detective. One day while her big sister was spending ages applying makeup and lipstick Vanessa went outside looking to uncover crimes.

To her surprise Vanessa found a bunch of keys on the driveway. They were attached to a watermelon shaped keyring. Vanessa also saw an unfamiliar motorbike. 'These are important clues', mumbled Vanessa. But before she could try and unlock the motorbike with the keys, her sister's boyfriend snatched them from her.

Now Vanessa knew why her sister had put on the sparkling earrings and necklace!

What am I?

- You find me . . .

- I can . . .

- An important thing about me is . . .

- When you look at me, you can see . . .

Example: 'You find me in the kitchen. I can cook food. An important thing about me is that I get hot. When you look at me, you can see a handle and lid. I am a . . .'

Noun Cards

glasses	purse
phone	fridge
elephant	pen
boots	watch
spoon	umbrella
clock	book
bike	T.V.

bed	hat
sandals	cat
spoon	train
doll	laptop
suitcase	tiger
magazine	toothbrush
flea	treasure
gravy	waterfall

marshmallow	kite
elbow	astronaut
computer	dentist
toad	professor
costume	tadpole
airport	beetle
compass	castle

shell	bridge
ambulance	factory
noodles	shampoo
supermarket	wheelchair
pancake	keyboard
swimming pool	watering can
mirror	earth

Verb Cards

creep	howl
chew	bounce
stroke	tug
splash	yell
tumble	drown
punch	work

grumble	chat
feed	nibble
dream	hatch
hop	select
shut	remove
remember	collect

salute	concentrate
shrug	donate
measure	decide
steal	protect
agree	collect
curse	daydream

Adjectives

cute	funny
lazy	weak
round	smooth
confused	clumsy
stinky	bossy
kind	worried

gigantic	dangerous
foggy	scruffy
salty	proud
honest	invisible
filthy	clever
flexible	sharp

perfect	spicy
sensible	worn out
weary	hilarious
difficult	disgusting
favourite	invisible
miserable	silent

Blank Cards to Add Additional Words

Nouns

Verbs

Adjectives

 Clue Cards

Clues for nouns: things that I can see and touch	
What can it do? What can you do with it? 	Describe what you see (important things). 
Where could you find it? 	Who uses it? 
When could you use this? 	

Clues for verbs: something that you can do

Use the best clue from the options below

Where would you do this?	Who or what does this?

When would you do this?	Think of another word that is a bit like this

Clues for adjectives: words to describe things

It can be used to describe … and …	Think of another word that is a bit like this
  e.g.: 'cute': cat and monkey	

Clues for any word

What kind of thing is it?	What is important about this word?

Word Spinner

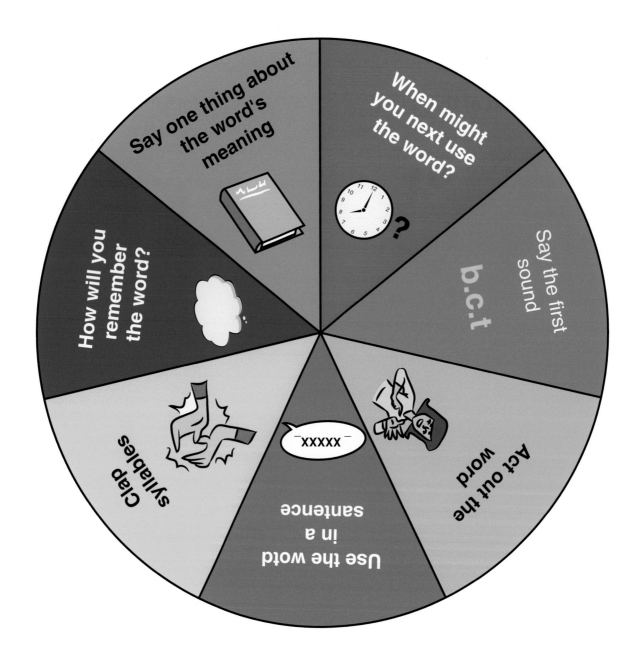

Space Race

Start

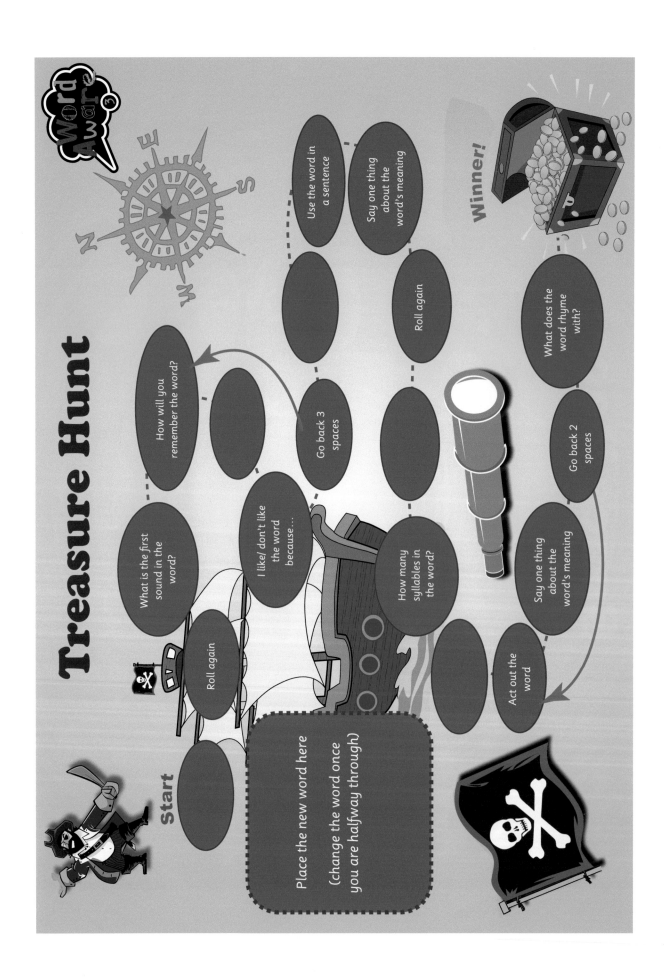

Treasure Hunt

Winner!

Start

Place the new word here
(change the word once
you are halfway through)

Use the word in a sentence

Say one thing about the word's meaning

Roll again

What does the word rhyme with?

How will you remember the word?

Go back 3 spaces

Go back 2 spaces

What is the first sound in the word?

I like/ don't like the word because…

How many syllables in the word?

Say one thing about the word's meaning

Roll again

Act out the word

Under the sea

Start

Roll again

What is the first sound in the word?

Say one thing about the word's meaning

How many syllables in the word?

Go back 3 spaces

I like/ don't like the word because...

How will you remember the word?

Roll again

Say one thing about the word's meaning

Go back 2 spaces

Act out the word

What does the word rhyme with?

Winner!

Place the new word here (change the word once you are halfway through)

Learn a Word Game

Beetle game

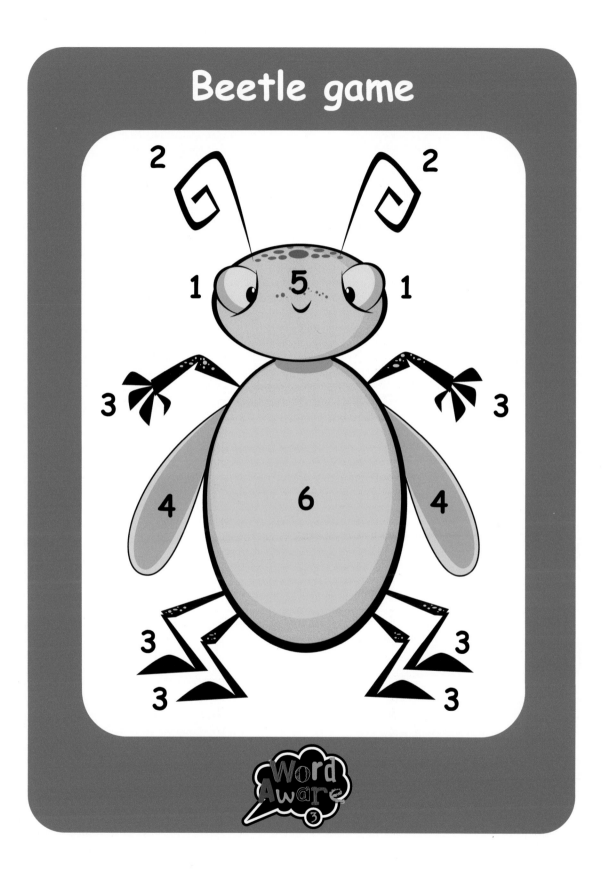

Beetle game instructions

Place the new word here

(change the word once you are halfway through)

Players must roll 6 and draw the body before any other body parts can be drawn.
Players must roll 5 and draw the head before the eyes and antennae.

Die roll	Instructions	Body part to draw
1	Give a word that goes with it or means something similar.	Eyes
2	Put the word in a sentence.	Antennae
3	Tell me one thing about the word's meaning.	Legs
4	What rhymes with it?	Wings
5	How many syllables does it have?	Head
6	What is the first sound?	Body

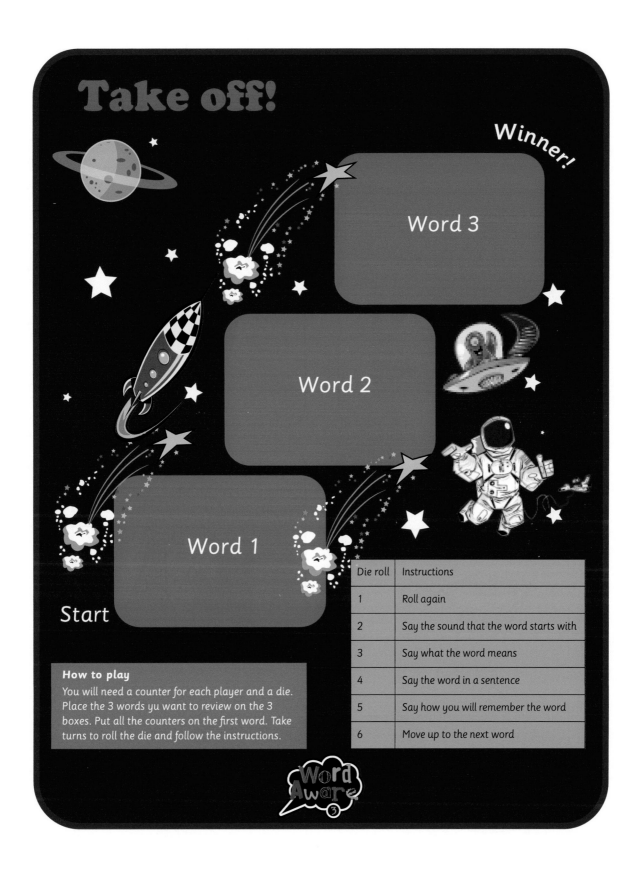

Take off!

Winner!

Word 3

Word 2

Word 1

Start

Die roll	Instructions
1	Roll again
2	Say the sound that the word starts with
3	Say what the word means
4	Say the word in a sentence
5	Say how you will remember the word
6	Move up to the next word

How to play
You will need a counter for each player and a die. Place the 3 words yu want to review on the 3 boxes. Put all the counters on the first word. Take turns to roll the die and follow the instructions.

 **Linking the Words to the Class**

What Shall We Do Today?

Give the new word to the class teacher.

Put it on the class Word Wall.

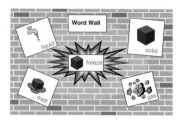

Add the word into the Word Pot and take it into class.

Go into class and tell the **class** about the word we have been learning.

Listen out for the word in class. Your teacher and other adults will use the word.

Go into class and tell the **teacher** about the word we have been learning.

Show the class the Word Wizard we did today. We can teach the class the action.

Shaboo Cards

Shaboo cards

Act It

Read the word on the card silently. Act out the meaning of the word. No noises or air spelling of word is allowed.

Don't Say It

Read the word on the card silently. Without saying the word on the card, define the word to help others guess the correct word.

Draw It

Read the word on the card silently. Draw a picture on the board that shows the meaning of the word. No speaking, gesturing or writing letters.

Use It

This time you can say the word. Use the word in a sentence showing that you understand the meaning.

This Word Is a Bit like...

Read the word on the card silently. Without saying the word on the card, provide a similar word. Start by saying 'this word on the card is a bit like …' If they do not guess, then add 'this word is a bit like that other word but…'

Something Special

Without saying the word on the card, say something special or unique about it. It might be its spelling, what it means, when it can be used or why you like. Think hard about why it is special.

Take another card and earn double points when you roll the dice

Lose all points. Do not take another card.

Word Fortune Teller

1 — Say one thing about the word's meaning

2 — How many syllables does it have?

3 — What word is a bit like this word?

4 — What does it rhyme with?

5 — What does the word mean?

6 — Act out the word

7 — Use the word in a sentence

8 — What does it start with?

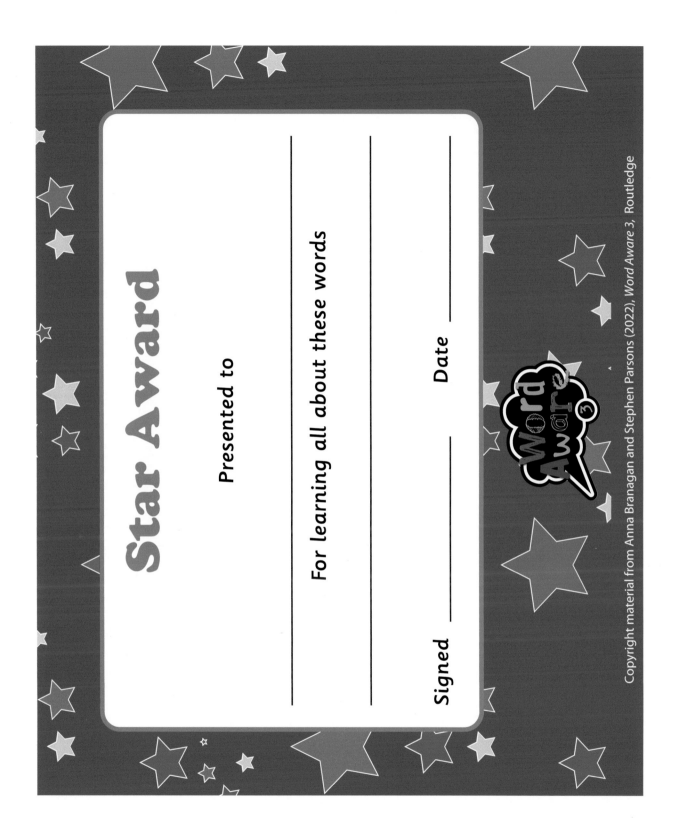

Star Award

Presented to

For learning all about these words

Date

Signed

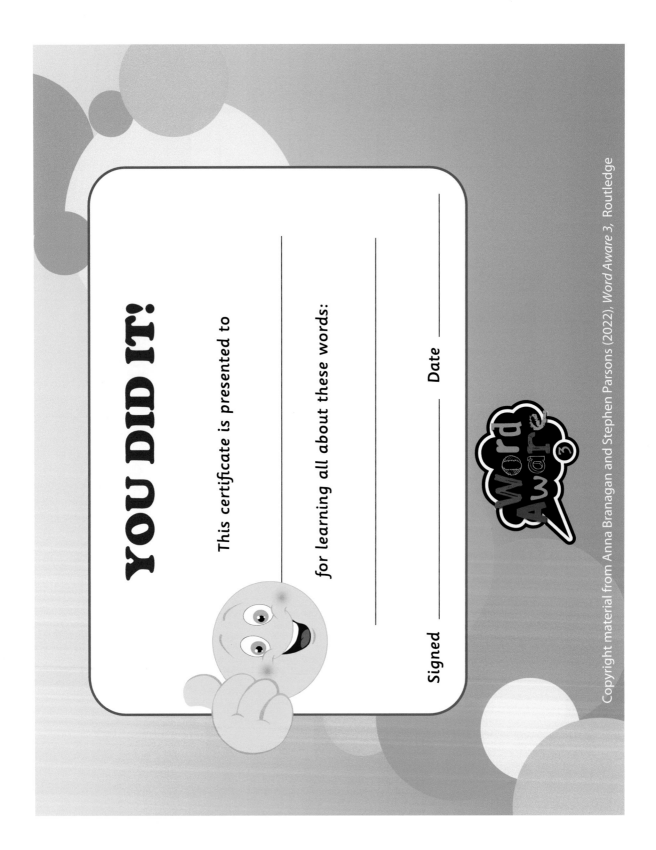

YOU DID IT!

This certificate is presented to

_____

for learning all about these words:

_____

Signed _____ Date _____

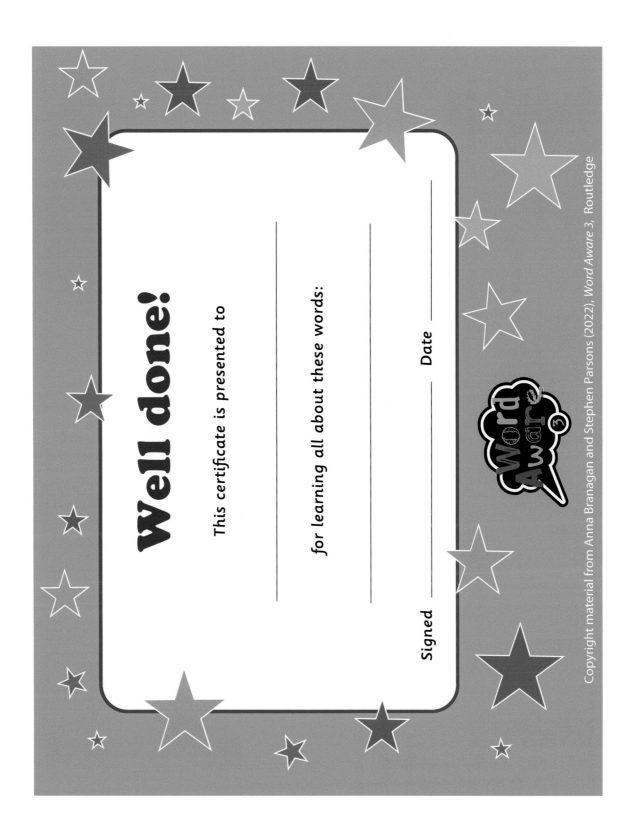

Well done!

This certificate is presented to

_____

for learning all about these words:

_____

_____

Signed _____

Date _____

Attendance and Intervention Record

	Week 1			Week 2		Week 3	Review last 5 words
Words introduced	Word:	Word:		Word:	Word:	Word:	
Word learning skills	☐ Compound words ☐ Looking at the beginning of words ☐ Applying word learning skills		☐ Looking at the ends of words ☐ Multiple meanings ☐ Definition skills				
Children	Date:	Date:		Date:	Date:	Date:	Date:

Teacher Feedback

As you know, a group of children from your class have been coming out of class to learn some new words. The words that have been taught recently in the group are:

The word learning skills we have been focusing on recently are ☐ **compound words,** ☐ **prefixes** ☐ **suffixes** ☐ **multiple meanings and** ☐ **defining words.**

What effect have you noticed the group has had on each child? Please tick

Child's name	I haven't noticed any benefit.	I have noticed some benefit	I have noticed significant benefit

What have you noticed? Have you heard the children say the words? Have they used them in their writing? Have they applied word learning skills in the classroom? Have any of these skills any knock-on effects?

If a child is not making progress, then reflect on why. Consider changes to the group, how the group links with the class, increasing vocabulary teaching in the class or advice from specialists.

Assessment of Word Knowledge

Child's name		Year group		Date	

☐ **Before Intervention**   ☐ **After Intervention**

Words	Child rating of word knowledge			If a child says they know the word, ask them 'What do you know about this word?' If they give an answer which only gives partial information (a score of 1) prompt with, 'Use the word in a sentence.' Mark (SP) to indicate 'sentence prompt is used'. Write what the child says here.	Score
	Never heard of it	Heard of it but not sure what it means	Knows what it means		
					/3
					/3
					/3
					/3
					/3

	Total score: /15

Scoring criteria

Never heard of it or has heard of it but unable to provide any further relevant information. Score 0 if the child can define another meaning of the word but not the one targeted here.	0
Gives some information about the word but it is missing important points.	1
Most key information provided, but some points left out, so may still be a bit general or mildly confusing. If they cannot fully explain the word but can use it in a sentence, then the maximum score is 2.	2
Clear definition and unlikely to be confused with another word.	3

 **Intervention Resources**

Assessment of Word Learning Skills

Name:	Date:

All resources are on pages 138–140. Read the words to the child if they experience any difficulty.

Area	Task	Target answer	Score
1. Speech sounds in a word *Resources: none required*	Example: say: 'If I say the word "butterfly" the first sound is "b". I can clap out the syllables "bu-tter-fly" and it would be 3 claps. I can think of a silly word that rhymes with it: "mutterfly".'		
	What is the first sound in the word 'donkey'?	d	/1
	How many claps (syllables) does 'donkey' have?	2	/1
	Make up a silly rhyme for the word 'donkey'.	wonkey, lonkey etc.	/1
	What is the first sound in the word 'caterpillar'?	c	/1
	How many claps does 'caterpillar' have? (syllables)	4	/1
	Make up a silly rhyme with the word 'caterpillar'.	saterpillar. materpillar etc.	/1
	What is the first sound in the word 'ant?	a	/1
	How many claps does 'ant' have? (syllables)	1	/1
	Make up a silly rhyme with the word 'ant'.	tant, lant etc.	/1
2. Compound words *Resources: see page 138*	1 Example: Show the printed word 'lipstick'. Say: 'If we look at this word together it says 'lipstick'. In this word I can see two other words inside the word. I can see 'lip' and 'stick'.	2 Example: Now show the printed word 'parent'. Read it aloud and then say, 'in this word I cannot break it down into two smaller words'.	
	Show the words 'caveman', 'burglar', 'bathroom', 'marble', 'picture', 'football', 'downstairs' and 'pebble'. Say, 'Look at the words. Do any of these words have little words inside the words you can see? What are the words?'	Score 1 for identifying each of these: foot, ball, cave, man, bath, room, down or stairs. Score -1 (minus 1) each time child incorrectly identifies other words. If total is a minus number, just score 0.	/6

Area	Task	Target answer	Score
3. Suffixes (parts at the ends of words) *Resources: see page 138*	Example: Say 'Look at these sentences: "They are jumping on the trampoline" and "They jumped on the trampoline." If I look closely, I can see (and hear) that one sentence has "ing" in "jumping" so that one is happening now. The other sentence has "ed" in "jumped" and so that has already happened.		
	"She is walking" and " 'She walked". Tell me the difference between these two sentences.'	Score 1 if they are able to describe the difference between the two sentences, e.g. 'This one is now and in that one she has finished walking.'	/1
	Say 'Look at these sentences: "The cat sat on the chair" and "The cats sat on the chair." Tell me the difference between these two sentences.'	Score 1 if they are able to describe the difference between the two sentences, e.g.: one sentence is about one cat and the other is about multiple cats	/1
4. Prefixes (parts at the beginning of words) *Resources: see page 139*	Look at the words 'zip' and 'unzip'. Ask, 'How are they different?' If they say 'There is an "un" ' then ask 'how does that change their meaning?'	Score 1 if they can say that 'zip' is to 'zip up' and unzip is to undo. Demonstration is acceptable.	/1
	Look at the words 'play' and 'replay'. Ask 'How are they different?' If they say 'There is a "re" ' then ask 'how does that change the meaning?'	Score 1 if they can say that 'replay means you have to play it again'.	/1
5. Multiple meanings *Resources: see page 139*	Example: Say 'The word "bat" can mean different things. Sometimes it means something you use to hit a ball, or it can be an animal that can fly.'		
	Look at these words: 'banana', 'puddle', 'wave', 'scared'. Do any of these words have more than one meaning? Further point if can give any indication of the two meanings of 'wave'.	Identifies 'wave' (and no other word) (1 point). Can say the 2 meanings (1 point)	/2
	Look at these words: 'trip', 'roof', 'pebble', 'lizard'. Do any of these words have more than one meaning? Further point if can give any indication of the two meanings of 'trip'.	Identifies 'trip' (and no other word) (1 point). Can say the 2 meanings (1 point)	/2

Area	Task	Target answer	Score
6. Definitions *Resources: see page 140. Keep the pictures hidden from the child's view.* *Use the scoring criteria on page 141.*	Example: pick up the picture of the egg but don't show it to the child. Say 'I am going to describe it to you. You need to guess what it is. It's something you eat. You can boil it or fry it. A chicken lays it. At Easter you get chocolate ones.'		
	Say: 'Now it's your turn. Pick one of the cards. Don't tell me what it is. Your job is to give me clues so that I can guess what it is.' Write the child's description here:		/3
	Say: 'Now give me clues about the next word, but don't tell me what it is.' Write the child's description here:		/3
	Say: 'Now the last one. Give me clues about the word, but don't tell me what it is.' Write the child's description here:		/3
		Total	/32

Word Learning Skills Assessment Resources

1. Compound words/and non-compound words

lipstick	parent
caveman	burglar
bathroom	marble
picture	football
downstairs	pebble

2. Suffixes (parts at the end of the word)

They are jumping on the trampoline.	They jumped on the trampoline.

She is walking.	She walked.

The cat sat on the chair.	The cats sat on the chair.

3. Prefixes (parts at the beginning of the word)

zip	unzip

play	replay

4. Multiple meanings and non-examples

banana	puddle	wave	scared

trip	roof	pebble	lizard

5. Simple definitions

Cut out each of these

egg

grumpy

stroke

farm

Definitions scoring criteria

Never heard of it or has heard of it but unable to provide any further relevant information. Score 0 if the child can define another meaning of the word but not the one targeted here.	0
Gives some information about the word but it is missing important points.	1
Most key information provided, but some points left out, so may still be a bit general. If they cannot fully explain the word but can use it in a sentence, then the maximum score is 2.	2
Clear definition and unlikely to be confused with another word.	3

Scoring examples

	0	1	2	3
farm	We went there on a school trip.	It's got chickens.	Where the animals live.	It's where animals live, like cows and horses. Where food is grown.
stroke	That's cute.	Cats like it.	Like when you pat the dog.	You do this with a cat and dog. They like it. You keep moving your hand gently.
grumpy	I'm grumpy.	I don't like grumpy people.	Not a nice feeling.	In a bad mood. A little bit cross.

Chapter 5. Staff Training Guide

In a busy school it is easy to skip over training, but it is essential if the intervention is to be effective. The resources are all provided to make the training as time-efficient as possible, and it should take approximately one and a half hours. It is advised that **all** school staff who are involved in the intervention are trained together, including the class teacher and the Special Educational Needs Coordinator. This will ensure that all fully understand each other's roles, which then lays the foundations for close teamwork.

The training provided is a quick overview. Ahead of the training it is strongly advised that one person reads the book and is familiar with the approach, so they can answer questions. Other staff are encouraged to read the book also.

By the time this training is delivered it is presumed that target children have been identified, staff allocated, and the twice-weekly sessions timetabled.

PowerPoint slides and a video recording of the authors talking through the presentation are available on the companion website which accompanies this book. Details of how to access it are available on page i. All you need to do is gather around a screen together and collect a few resources.

During the training, access to a copy of this book is required. This will allow staff members to become more familiar with the approach and the resources in their entirety.

Whilst the presentation and the slides show the required resources, it is easier for attendees to visualise what they need to do when they have sight of real paper copies and resources. Almost all of the printed resources will be used as part of the intervention, so the printing is not wasted.

Prior to the training, copy from the book/print from the companion website the following resources. On the companion website these are all in one section ready to print, titled 'Resources to Accompany Training'. They are listed in the order that they are referred to in the training:

1. 'Training PowerPoint slides' (companion website only)
2. Whole class vocabulary planning sheet, page 67 in Chapter 4
3. Fridge Words, page 68 in Chapter 4
4. Visual timetables on page 76 in Chapter 4
5. Warm-up games; choose one, pages 37–39 in Chapter 4
6. Word Wizard, page 79 in Chapter 4
7. Songs, pages 80–82 in Chapter 4
8. 'Be a word detective' bookmark, page 97 in Chapter 4
9. Board games, pages 118–125 in Chapter 4
10. 'Rate your word knowledge', page 84 in Chapter 4
11. Symbols for 'carbohydrates', 'nutrients', 'digestion', 'protein' and 'evidence', page 148 in this chapter
12. Attendance and intervention record sheet, page 132 in Chapter 4

13. Teacher feedback, page 133 in Chapter 4

14. Assessment of word knowledge, page 134 in Chapter 4

15. Assessment of word learning skills, pages 135–137 in Chapter 4

16. Whole class teaching to support vulnerable word learners, page 146 in this chapter

17. What you need to know to support word learning, page 147 in this chapter

18. Building a vocabulary team, pages 27–28 in Chapter 2.

You will also need

- some cloth or an eye mask to play the blindfold game

- dice and counters for the board games.

If not made already, take a look at 'How to make a Word Pot,' page 83 in Chapter 4.

When you are ready, go to the companion website at www.routledge.com/cw/speechmark and watch the authors present an overview.

Whole Class Teaching to Support Vulnerable Word Learners

Planning

- Teacher identifies key 'Goldilocks' words to teach to the class.
- The teacher Identifies which of these words the group will pre-teach. Add any 'Anchor' words if they are needed. Write definitions of these words on the 'Fridge Words' for the group facilitator.

Teaching

- Teacher identifies 'Goldilocks' words **to the whole class**, using a Word Wizard (see page 79). This should take 5 minutes.
- Make teaching as multi-sensory as possible; act out ways of walking, moving and speaking, use multiple images to enhance meaning, provide opportunities for hands on learning.
- Place taught word in the Word Pot (see page 83) and on the Word Wall (see page 40).
- The group facilitator will add any additional words the group has been learning to both the Word Pot and the Word Wall. All words can be reviewed by the whole class.

Activating and reviewing taught words

- Use taught words in context as much as you can, linking words with practical activities. This applies to both the words learnt by the whole class and any additional words taught in the group. Remember these children need to hear words more times than their peers.
- Link the new word back to a simple word that they are familiar with. Highlight when one word would be used and not the other.
- Encourage children to write the word: recording in a personal dictionary, writing in sentences or a mind map
- Support the targeted children to use the learnt words in the classroom and at home. Praise them when they do. Encourage the group children to contribute to whole class discussions about the words' meanings.
- Talk about words on the Word Wall and in Word Pot.

Independent word learning strategies

- Encourage all children to identify words they do not know e.g.: children can underline unknown words in a worksheet, talk about unknown words found in books.
- Encourage children to look within words for parts that they recognise.
- Look out for prefixes. Make sure everyone is looking out for 'un' and 're'.
- Talk about how word endings affect the meaning.
- Talk about words with multiple meanings.
- Use the clue cards on pages 115–117. Use these to help define new words.

Get children excited about words

- Get all children excited by words by playing word games and talking about words.
- Encourage families to play word games (see pages 69–73).

For further ideas on developing a whole school vocabulary approach, refer to *Word Aware 1*, 2nd edition (Parsons & Branagan, 2022).

Be a word detective!

I can find words made up of other words,
e.g. snow/ball

I can find words that start with prefixes like 'un' and 're',
e.g. unfair, redo

I know how the end of a word changes what it means,
e.g. cat/cats, walk/ walking

I look out for words that have more than one meaning,
e.g. mummy

What You Need to Know to Support Word Learning

- Word learning needs to be fun!
- Work as a team.
- Words chosen should be really useful.
- Make sure you have clear definitions that use simple words.
- Maximise learning, by linking class, group and home together.
- Pre-teach the word in the group so when the children take the word into class, they can access whole class teaching and learn more.
- Teach 'Goldilocks' words to the whole class.
- When children are learning new words, they need to hear them lots of times, so use the word many times throughout the session, in the classroom and at home.
- Come back and review words from time to time, otherwise words will be forgotten.
- Teach children how to learn words too, as most words are learnt independently.

Symbols for Use in Training Session

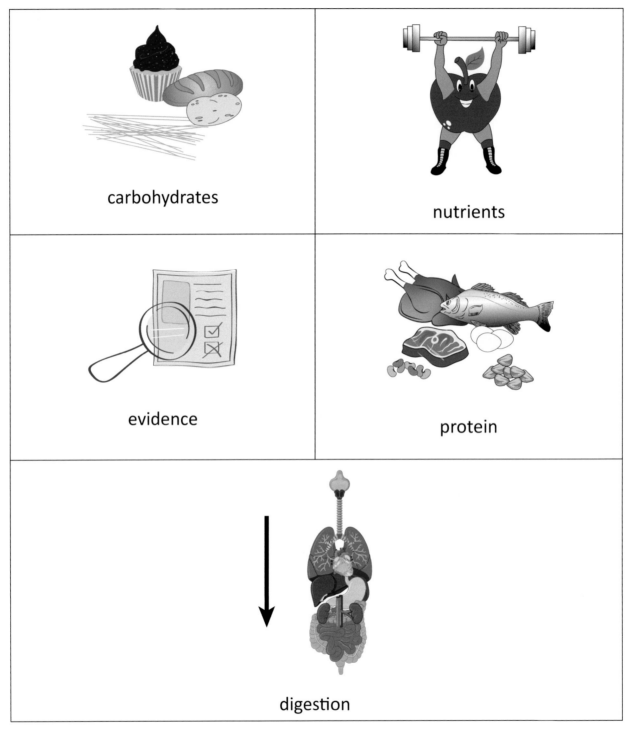

carbohydrates

nutrients

evidence

protein

digestion

Reference

Parsons, S. & Branagan, A. (2022). *Word Aware 1: Teaching Vocabulary Across the Day, Across the Curriculum*, 2nd edition. Abingdon, Oxon: Routledge.

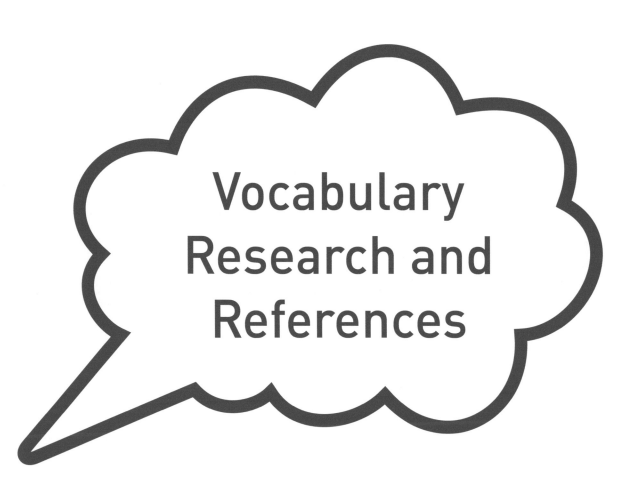

Vocabulary Research and References

Chapter 6. Vocabulary Research and References

As the evidence base for the principles and general impact of vocabulary difficulties are covered in *Word Aware 1*, 2nd edition (Parsons & Branagan, 2022) the research outlined here is specifically focussed on supporting the vocabulary needs of those with additional learning needs. You can access the 'Introduction' chapter from *Word Aware 1*, 2nd edition from the Speechmark companion website www.routledge.com/cw/speechmark.

Vocabulary in the Classroom

Support for children with weak vocabulary skills needs to start in the classroom.

In recent years there has been an upsurge in the interest in vocabulary. In a survey (Oxford University Press, 2018) 69% of the primary school teachers said, 'that they think the number of pupils with limited vocabulary is either increasing or significantly increasing in their schools compared to a few years ago'. The same survey found that according to teacher report, on average 49% of Year 1 pupils have a limited vocabulary to the extent that it affects their learning (Oxford University Press, 2018).

This is of concern as the Department for Education (DfE, England, 2017) found those with poor spoken language skills (including vocabulary) are at great risk in literacy but even greater risk in mathematics: 'children who are behind in language development at age five are six times less likely to reach the expected standard in English at age eleven, and 11 times less likely to achieve the expected level in maths' (DfE, 2017).

Researchers such as Ford-Connors and Paratore (2015) highlight 'students who enter classrooms with a low store of vocabulary knowledge are unlikely to acquire complex knowledge through simple exposure'. And so, we need to take action

Fortunately, in more recent years there is a growing consensus around what good vocabulary instruction should consist of in the classroom. It is perhaps best summarised by Graves (2015) as a rich language environment, direct teaching of word meanings, strategy instruction, and supporting students' word consciousness (i.e. awareness that words are important). *Word Aware 1*, 2nd edition (Parsons & Branagan, 2022) outlines a comprehensive approach to developing vocabulary which will support most word learners, including those with some level of vulnerability. Even with enhancements the classroom environment may not support all learners and McGregor et al. (2020) point out that using the methods of instruction highlighted above is challenging for children with Developmental Language Disorder.

Who Has Vocabulary Needs?

In recent years, a consensus view has been reached regarding how language impairment is viewed (Bishop et al., 2017) and the term Developmental Language Disorder (DLD) adopted internationally. Children with DLD frequently have difficulties with vocabulary as a key component of this condition

(Kan & Windsor, 2010). McGregor et al., 2013 found that children with DLD have issues with the number of words they know (breadth) and how much they know about these known words (depth).

Cuskelly et al. (2016) report that people with Down Syndrome have difficulties with receptive vocabulary, whereas Laws et al., 2014 found that children and young people with Down Syndrome had comparative strengths in receptive vocabulary in relation to nonverbal abilities but had expressive difficulties and issues with depth of knowledge. Smith et al. (2020) found that children with Down Syndrome did not transfer learning from intervention groups to functional contexts.

Vocabulary knowledge may not be thought of as an obvious component of dyslexia, but Adlof and Hogan (2018) found that 55% of children with dyslexia could be classified as having DLD, a condition in which vocabulary needs are very common. Additionally, there were children with dyslexia who did not fit the criteria for DLD who exhibited significantly poorer vocabulary than their typically developing peers. Children with dyslexia are also at risk of slower vocabulary growth as they are not exposed to rich vocabulary via wide reading.

Although not widely researched, Korrel et al. (2017) highlight that many children with ADHD have language difficulties, incorporating vocabulary learning needs.

Not all children with the above conditions will have vocabulary needs, but learners with these conditions should be monitored closely. There will also be children with special educational needs without any diagnostic label who require support with vocabulary learning.

English as an Additional Language Learners/ English Language Learners

English as an Additional Language (EAL)/English Language Learners (ELL) can of course be diagnosed with any of the conditions highlighted above. In many industrial nations there are also high rates of social deprivation in immigrant, bilingual communities, which will impact on vocabulary. Vocabulary needs have been linked to social deprivation (Biemiller, 2005). There are, however, specific vocabulary learning issues when the school and home language differ. Gallagher et al. (2019) found that 'emergent bilingual students are less likely to benefit from incidental instruction of academic vocabulary words, which supports previous literature on the crucial role of explicit vocabulary instruction'. Robust vocabulary teaching in the classroom will support most EAL/ELL but their vocabulary development should be closely monitored. The home environment (monolingual and bilingual) typically uses much less challenging vocabulary than school where rich and academic language are the norm. Difficulties with language acquisition may therefore not be obvious to families.

Word Selection

Justice et al. (2014) found that traditional Speech and Language Therapy targets low level vocabulary that is not relevant to the curriculum. Words being taught in isolation outside of the classroom create issues with low numbers of repetition, lack of authentic context and transfer from the group to the classroom. Instead, Justice et al. (2014) recommend that therapy should include functional vocabulary targets that will help children succeed in the academic curriculum as well as social circumstances.

Lowe et al. (2017) reviewed the literature for adolescents and came to the conclusion that functional curriculum- related words in the classroom context should be the focus of intervention.

This concurs with the Educational Endowment Foundation who, after reviewing the literature, stated that approaches which aim to improve spoken vocabulary 'work best when they are related to current content being studied in school, and when they involve active and meaningful use of any new vocabulary' (2019).

Types of Intervention

Small groups are the most common intervention for at-risk word learners. Steele and Mills (2011) recommend small groups over individual sessions as they facilitate more discussion and learning. When linked to the classroom small groups can be particularly effective for at risk students as words can be introduced and then reviewed in the classroom (Seven et al., 2020). Coyne et al. (2019) found similar for at-risk kindergarten students, who learnt the specifically taught words well enough to catch up with their peers on the specific word measure. Some caution needs to be applied as for some groups, such as children with Down Syndrome, words that have been effectively learnt in the group may not transfer to more functional contexts (Smith et al., 2020).

Much of the research is with small groups run by Speech and Language Therapists/Speech-Language Pathologists or teachers, but Joffe et al. (2019) found that teaching assistant-run groups supported secondary students with weak language in learning vocabulary. At the other end of the age spectrum Fricke et al. (2013) used teaching assistants to teach vocabulary to 4- to 5-year-olds with weak language skills. Both of these studies targeted language more broadly than vocabulary. They both emphasise the need for extensive training and support if the intervention is to be effective.

Intervention Components

Much of the intervention that is used in this book stems from the study by Parsons et al. (2005) which taught curriculum-related mathematical vocabulary to children with severe DLD. In this study words were selected from the curriculum and introduced in individual sessions before being transferred back to the classroom. Features such as the 'Word Wizard', Word Wall, 'Fridge Words' and games which are part of *Word Aware 3* are all derived from this study.

The study by St John and Vance (2014) shares many similarities with the Parsons et al. (2005) study, but the approach was applied to children with low language abilities (including EAL/ELL). Curriculum nouns were pre-taught in structured small groups with visual supports and interactive review activities. Both this and the Parsons et al. (2005) study were found to be effective and children learnt the taught words.

Both the Parsons et al. (2005) and St John and Vance (2014) studies use a combined semantic and phonological approach as a key part of teaching new words. The phonological component includes highlighting initial phoneme, syllable, rime and saying the word aloud. The semantic element includes a simple definition, expanding children's knowledge and connecting that with children's existing knowledge. Lowe et al. (2017) conducted a systematic review of the literature for adolescents and found that the strongest evidence for effectiveness was for a combined phonological-semantic approach.

Good et al. (2015) used a morphological intervention for children with DLD, aged about 8 years. This involved teaching prefixes and suffixes. They found it to be effective for vocabulary, and also spelling, but not reading.

With secondary students, Spencer et al. (2017) combined semantic and phonological approach with additional focus on morphology, as well as adding concept mapping and experiential learning.

Others such as Dyson et al. (2018) found that for 6- to 9-year-olds with weak language skills, student-friendly definitions, visual supports and multiple examples were important components of the intervention. Van Berkel-van Hoof (2019) found that signing helped children with DLD learn new words.

For bilingual learners, Restrepo et al. (2013) found that both monolingual and bilingual instruction were effective, but bilingual a bit more. The intervention included hands-on activities that allow the child to hear, repeat, say, define and use the words multiple times, which are hallmarks of the semantic-phonological approach.

Word Finding Difficulties

Ebbels et al. (2012) identify word finding difficulties (WFD) as being 'characterized by hesitations, false starts, fillers (such as "um", "er"), empty words (such as "thingy"), and circumlocutions (where the child describes the word without accessing it)'. In lay terms, word finding difficulties are those 'tip of the tongue' experiences when the speaker cannot quite recall a word. WFD are common in children with DLD.

Wilson et al. (2015) argue that word finding and word learning are likely to be related. They hypothesise that words that are difficult to recall are because they have not been learnt to adequate depth. To learn words well, children need more exposures and more structured learning opportunities. The word learning activities outlined in *Word Aware 3* are very similar to those that support children with word finding difficulties. Specialist assessment is recommended, but activities in this book may be used as a first response to support children with word finding difficulties.

Impact

Both Parsons et al. (2005) and St John and Vance (2014) were successful interventions, as children learnt the targeted words effectively. However, in neither of these studies was there a change in children's performance on standardised vocabulary measures. Similarly, in Coyne et al.'s (2019) study there was only change on the taught words. The vocabulary typically measured on standardised measures is general and differs from the curriculum words taught. To show change on standardised measures it is postulated that interventions will need to be long-term and intense.

The vocabulary demands of the curriculum are immense, and for learners with additional needs it is not possible to close the vocabulary gap via direct teaching. The aim is instead to teach enough important words that this group of learners is able to access whole class teaching, thus mitigating the impact of the vocabulary needs.

References

Adlof, S. M. & Hogan, T. P. (2018). Understanding dyslexia in the context of developmental language disorders. *Language, Speech and Hearing Services in Schools*, 49: 4.

Biemiller, A. (2005). Size and sequence in vocabulary development: Implications for choosing words for primary grade vocabulary instruction. In A. Hiebert & M. Kamil (Eds.), *Teaching and Learning Vocabulary: Bringing Research to Practice* (pp. 223–242). Mahwah, NJ: Lawrence Erlbaum Associates.

Bishop, D.V., Snowling, M. J., Thompson, P.A., Greenhalgh, T. & CATALISE Consortium (2017). Phase 2 of CATALISE: a multinational and multidisciplinary Delphi consensus study of problems with language development: Terminology. *Journal of Child Psychology and Psychiatry*, 58: 1068–1080.

Coyne, M. D., McCoach, D. B., Ware, S., Austin, C. R., Loftus-Rattan, S. M. & Baker, D. L. (2019). Racing against the vocabulary gap: Matthew effects in early vocabulary instruction and intervention. *Exceptional Children*, 85:2, 163–179.

Cuskelly, M., Povey, J. & Jobling, A. (2016). Trajectories of development of receptive vocabulary in individuals with Down Syndrome. *Journal of Policy and Practice in Intellectual Disabilities*, 13: 111–119.

Ford-Connors, E. & Paratore, J. (2015). Vocabulary instruction in fifth grade and beyond: Sources of word learning and productive contexts for development. *Review of Educational Research*, 85:1, 50–91.

Dyson, H., Solity, J., Best, W. & Hulme, C. (2018). Effectiveness of a small-group vocabulary intervention programme: evidence from a regression discontinuity design. *International Journal of Language & Communication Disorders*, 53: 947–958.

Ebbels, S., Nicoll, H. & Clark, B. (2012). Effectiveness of semantic therapy for word-finding difficulties in pupils with persistent language impairments: A randomized control trial. *International Journal of Language and Communication Disorders*, 47: 35–51.

Fricke, S., Bowyer-Crane, C., Haley, A.J., Hulme, C. & Snowling, M. J. (2013). Efficacy of language intervention in the early years. *Journal of Child Psychology and Psychiatry*, 54, 280–290.

Gallagher, M.A., Taboada Barber, A., Beck, J. S. & Buehl, M. M. (2019). Academic vocabulary: Explicit and incidental instruction for students of diverse language backgrounds, *Reading & Writing Quarterly*, 35:2, 84–102.

Good, J.E., Lance, D.M. & Rainey J. (2015). The effects of morphological awareness training on reading, spelling, and vocabulary skills. *Communication Disorders Quarterly*, 36:3, 142–151.

Graves, M.F. (2015). Building a vocabulary program that really could make a significant contribution to students becoming college and career ready. In P.D. Pearson & E.H.

Hiebert (Eds.), *Research-based practices for Common Core literacy* (pp. 123–142). New York: Teachers College Press.

Joffe, V.L., Rixon, L. & Hulme, C. (2019). Improving storytelling and vocabulary in secondary school students with language disorder: a randomized controlled trial. *International Journal of Language & Communication Disorders*, 54: 656–672.

Justice, L.M., Schmitt, M.B., Murphy, K.A., Pratt, A. & Biancone, T. (2014). The 'robustness' of vocabulary intervention in the public schools: targets and techniques employed in speech–language therapy. *International Journal of Language & Communication Disorders*, 49, 288–303.

Kan, P. & Windsor, J. (2010). Word learning in children with primary language impairment: a meta-analysis. *Journal of Speech Language and Hearing Research*, 53, 739–756.

Korrel, H., Mueller, K.L., Silk, T., Anderson, V. & Sciberras, E. (2017). Research review: Language problems in children with Attention-Deficit Hyperactivity Disorder – a systematic meta-analytic review. *Journal of Child Psychology and Psychiatry*, 58, 640–654.

Laws, G. J., Briscoe, J., Ang, S. Y. Y., Brown, H., Hermena, E., & Kapikian, A. K. (2014). Receptive vocabulary and semantic knowledge in children with SLI and children with Down Syndrome. *Child Neuropsychology*, 21:4, 490–508.

Lowe, H., Henry, L., Muller, L-M. & Joffe, V. (2017). Vocabulary intervention for adolescents with language disorder: A systematic review. *International Journal of Language & Communication Disorders*, 53, 199–217.

McGregor, K.K., Oleson, J., Bahnsen, A. and Duff, D. (2013). Children with developmental language impairment have vocabulary deficits characterized by limited breadth and depth. International. *Journal of Language & Communication Disorders,* 48, 307–319.

McGregor, K. K., Van Horne, A., Curran, M., Cook, S. W. & Cole, R. (2020). The challenge of rich vocabulary instruction for children with developmental language disorder. https://doi.org/10.31219/osf.io/vru9b

Parsons, S. & Branagan, A. (2022). *Word Aware 1: Teaching Vocabulary Across the Day, Across the Curriculum*, 2nd edition. Abingdon, Oxon: Routledge.

Parsons, S., Law, J. & Gascoigne, M. (2005). Teaching receptive vocabulary to children with specific language impairment: a curriculum-based approach. *Child Language Teaching and Therapy*, 21:1, 39–59.

Restrepo, M. A., Morgan, G. P. & Thompson, M. S. (2013). The efficacy of a vocabulary intervention for dual-language learners with language impairment. *Journal of Speech, Language, and Hearing Research*, 56, 748–765.

Seven, Y., Hull, K., Madsen. K., Ferron, J., Peters-Sanders, L., Soto, X., Kelley. E. S. & Goldstein, H. (2020). Classwide extensions of vocabulary intervention improve learning of academic vocabulary by preschoolers. *Journal of Speech, Language and Hearing Research*, 63:1.

Smith, E., Hokstad, S. & Nɪ ss, K. B. (2020) Children with Down syndrome can benefit from language interventions; Results from a systematic review and meta-analysis. *Journal of Communication Disorders*, 85.

Spencer, S., Clegg, J., Lowe, H. & Stackhouse, J. (2017), Increasing adolescents' depth of understanding of cross-curriculum words: an intervention study. *International Journal of Language & Communication Disorders,* 52: 652–668.

Steele, S. C. & Mills, M. T. (2011). Vocabulary intervention for school-age children with language impairment: A review of evidence and good practice. *Child Language Teaching and Therapy*, 27:3, 354–370.

St John, P. & Vance, M. (2014). Evaluation of a principled approach to vocabulary learning in mainstream classes. *Child Language Teaching and Therapy*, 30:3, 255–271.

van Berkel-van Hoof, L., Hermans, D., Knoors, H. & Verhoeven, L. (2019). Effects of signs on word learning by children with developmental language disorder. *Journal of Speech, Language and Hearing Research*, 62:6.

Wilson, J., Aldersley, A., Dobson, C., Edgar, S., Harding, C., Luckins, J., Wiseman, F. & Pring, T. (2015). The effectiveness of semantic therapy for the word finding difficulties of children with severe and complex speech, language and communication needs. *Child Language Teaching and Therapy*, 31:1, 7–17.

Web references

Department for Education (2017) https://www.gov.uk/government/news/new-education-and-skills-measures-announced (accessed 21 May 2021).

Education Endowment Foundation (2019) *Oral Language Interventions* https://educationendowmentfoundation.org.uk/evidence-summaries/teaching-learning-toolkit/oral-language-interventions/ (accessed 21 May 2021).

Oxford University Press (2018) *Why Closing the Word Gap Matters: Oxford Language Report* oxford.ly/wordgap (accessed 1 June 2021).